DEVILS TOWER NATIONAL MONUMENT IN WYOMING, U.S.A., IS MADE FROM IGNEOUS ROCK THAT FORMED FROM MAGMA FROM EARTH'S CENTER THAT COOLED MILLIONS OF YEARS AGO.

THE WAVE, LOCATED IN COYOTE BUTTES, ARIZONA, U.S.A., IS MADE OF CALCIFIED SANDSTONE DUNES.

# NATIONAL GEOGRAPHIC KiDS

# Absolute Expert

# ROCKS AND MINERALS

All the LATEST FACTS From the Field

Ruth Strother

With National Geographic Explorer
Dr. Sarah Stamps

NATIONAL GEOGRAPHIC
Washington, D.C.

# CONTENTS

FOREWORD by National Geographic
Explorer Dr. Sarah Stamps ............ 6

## CHAPTER 1

### Rock On, Earth! 8

EXPLORER INTRODUCTION .............. 10
Earth's Layers From the Inside Out ...14
Layer Stats ....................................... 16
Earth on the Move............................. 18
Under Pressure ................................ 20
What Is a Mineral?............................ 22
What Is a Rock? ............................... 23
The Rock Cycle.................................. 26
ROCK OUT! Make Your Own
    Volcano .......................................... 28

## CHAPTER 2

### A Kaleidoscope of Crystals and Minerals 30

EXPLORER INTRODUCTION ............. 32
7 Crystal Systems ............................. 35
From Crystal to Mineral ................... 37
Bold Building Blocks ......................... 37
Name That Mineral .......................... 38
Fireworks! ........................................ 39
Alphabet Soup.................................. 46
Classy Minerals................................ 48
Native Elements Fun Facts............... 49
Gemstones ....................................... 61
Modern Birthstones ......................... 62
ROCK OUT! Crystal Candy ................ 64

# CHAPTER 3

## Rocks Under Pressure 66

**EXPLORER INTRODUCTION** ............. 68

Igneous Rocks .................................... 70

Sedimentary Rocks ........................... 79

Metamorphic Rocks ......................... 86

Out-of-This-World Rocks.................. 89

Meteorite Stars ................................. 90

**ROCK OUT!** Sedimentary
  Cementing ..................................... 92

# CHAPTER 4

## Living With Rocks and Minerals 94

**EXPLORER INTRODUCTION** ............. 96

Arty Buildings and Building Art......... 98

Growing Strong and Healthy With
  Minerals ......................................... 101

Tools and Technology ....................... 102

**ROCK OUT!** Rock Paint!.................... 104

**GLOSSARY** .........................................106

**MORE READING** ...............................108

**INDEX** ...............................................109

**PHOTO CREDITS** ..............................111

DR. SARAH STAMPS

DR. STAMPS IN THE
FIELD IN KENYA

# FOREWORD

I spend much of my life exploring Earth in search of rocks. I'm a geophysicist at the Virginia Tech Department of Geosciences, and I study Earth by measuring things and collecting data. My specialty is geodesy, a branch of earth science that uses math to understand our planet. It's my job to figure out how fast Earth's surface is moving. To do this, I measure rocks with specialized Global Navigation Satellite Systems (GNSS) equipment that can detect rock movement within a millimeter—a movement that's only about the size of your pencil tip!

DR. STAMPS SETS UP EQUIPMENT IN UGANDA.

I measure the movement of all types of rocks: igneous rocks, metamorphic rocks, and sedimentary rocks. But you can't just pick up the rocks I measure because I measure bedrock, which is solid and lies below the loose materials of Earth such as gravel and soil. Bedrock and other materials form the upper part of Earth's crust, which is where almost all earthquakes occur. Figuring out how bedrock moves helps us understand where there is danger of an earthquake occurring.

How did I become a geophysicist? It started with an interest in environmental science when I was in third grade, which grew into a fascination with archaeology in high school. I was drawn to geophysics when I had the opportunity to participate in the University of Missouri at Rolla's Jackling Institute.

The institute was so exciting! Researchers there showed us an image of a fault, a crack in the earth, beneath the surface. The image was made by vibrating the ground and sending sound waves into Earth that bounced back along different layers of rock and sediment in the crust. I was amazed that scientists could use technology to look inside Earth. From that point forward, I dreamed of being a professor of geophysics. After earning a bachelor's degree in earth science and a Ph.D. in geophysics, and conducting postdoctoral research in geodesy and geodynamics, I succeeded in my dream.

Now I'm focused on discovering why continents break apart, how long-term plate tectonic movements influence present-day earthquakes, and what factors control volcanic eruptions. My team at Virginia Tech examines these topics and operates TZVOLCANO, an observatory in Tanzania, Africa. The observatory records the activity of the volcano Ol Doinyo Lengai with GNSS instruments. (See our real-time streaming positioning data at tzvolcano.chordsrt.com.)

This book introduces you to the foundations of earth science and is a great place to start to build your knowledge of the rocks and minerals that make up our amazing planet. I hope you enjoy exploring this book!

—Dr. Sarah Stamps

THE RED SANDSTONE OF
HORSESHOE BEND IN ANTELOPE
CANYON IN ARIZONA, U.S.A.

# CHAPTER 1

# ROCK ON, EARTH!

# INTRODUCTION

## WHAT COMES TO MIND WHEN YOU THINK OF A SCIENTIST AT WORK?

You might imagine someone in a laboratory wearing a white coat and safety glasses pouring smoking liquids into beakers.

DR. SARAH STAMPS

But a lot of scientists conduct their experiments and collect data outside of the laboratory. It's called working in the field. Basically, they take their "laboratory" to the subjects they're studying, such as volcanoes. One of the fun parts about working in the field is that scientists never know what to expect. And on a particular trip to Tanzania, on the east coast of Africa, we definitely had a surprise in store for us.

I was traveling with a team in Tanzania. Mountains towered all around us, and the land was wide open and peaceful.

As beautiful as it was, we couldn't just stand around and admire the view. Earthquakes had recently shaken the region, so we had a job to do. We were there to put three global positioning system (GPS) sensors into rock, so we could measure Earth's movements to figure out the motion of Earth's crust.

The GPS sensors detect radio signals that come from GNSS. The U.S.-operated GPS is one of many GNSS systems. Our team's GPS stations detect signals from at least four satellites. These signals give our team our exact position and the exact time of a signal's measurement. Then we keep measuring the GPS signals to determine our position and how that position moves over time.

Earthquakes weren't the only forces shaking the region. Many mountains in the area are actually volcanoes.

We were staying about 11 miles (18 km) from a volcano named Ol Doinyo Lengai, or "Mountain of God," by the Maasai, who are indigenous people of Tanzania. On our way to our field site, the volcano started erupting. It was a small eruption, but ash and gas shot high into the air with a loud *Boom!* It was thrilling to see and hear.

Our site was only 6 miles (10 km) from Ol Doinyo Lengai. Even though we were so close to an active volcano, we decided to stay and put in the sensors. We were concentrating on our work when we were startled by another loud *Boom!* Then boom after boom! Our ears were ringing, and some ash was drifting down on the other side of the mountain.

It was an incredible display of Earth in action. We were all nervous and a little afraid, but we continued working and got the job done.

THE MAASAI ARE INDIGENOUS PEOPLE OF TANZANIA.

OL DOINYO LENGAI MEANS "MOUNTAIN OF GOD" IN THE MAASAI LANGUAGE.

ASH AND GASES SPEW OUT FROM THE VOLCANO!

OL DOINYO LENGAI ERUPTS.

# THE UNIVERSE BEGAN WITH GAS, DUST, AND SPACE ROCKS.

**Scientists pieced together the story of the universe in part by measuring the age of rocks and meteorites.**

From all the information that has been collected, most scientists agree that a huge explosion they call the big bang occurred about 10 to 20 billion years ago. Scientists believe that the makings of the universe had been trapped in a space just a bit bigger than a period on this page. After the big bang, the universe grew and expanded quickly. A result of the big bang was a cloud of gas and dust that started drifting through space. Scientists call this cloud a solar nebula. With

gravity's help, the solar nebula collapsed into itself and started spinning. In the center of this swirling dust storm, which included the gases helium and hydrogen, pressure increased, the temperature rose, and our sun was born.

The sun's heat created a wind strong enough to blow lightweight elements that were left over from the sun's birth, such as helium and hydrogen, away from the solar nebula. These lighter elements came together around rocky cores, or centers, and became planets called gas giants. You know these planets. In order from the sun, they're Jupiter, Saturn, Uranus, and Neptune. The lighter elements also came together with bits of rock and metal to create comets, asteroids, and moons.

The force of gravity was so strong that the heavier rocks and metals that were left over in outer space from the sun's birth remained near the sun. It was at about this time that the rock and metal debris started playing a strange sort of bumper cars. They were orbiting the sun, hurtling through space, and crashing into one another at superhigh speeds. Unlike bumper cars, though, some of these space rocks collided with such

A NEBULA IN DEEP SPACE

MOLTEN ROCK POURS ONTO EARTH'S SURFACE.

force that they stuck together until they became big enough to be a rocky, or terrestrial, planet.

You know how when you're cold you might rub your hands together to warm up? This is called friction, and the force of one hand rubbing against the other creates heat. Crashing space rocks create friction, too. Imagine the heat created by the force of all those space rocks colliding. The heat was so high the rock that would eventually be called Earth melted. And guess what we call molten, or melted, rock? We call it magma when it's inside Earth and lava when it erupts from a volcano onto Earth's surface. Baby Earth started as a huge, ultra-heated, bubbling ball of magma!

Other terrestrial planets were being formed in the solar system during this time. You know these planets, too. In order from the sun, they are Mercury, Venus, and Mars. Earth is tucked in between Venus and Mars.

THE SOLAR SYSTEM AS WE KNOW IT TODAY STARTED AS GAS, DUST, AND ROCK.

Now that we know how the planets came to be, let's go back and visit Earth about 4.1 billion years ago. Earth has been an ultrahot mass during much of its life, but 500 million years after it started to form, Earth became even hotter, hot enough to melt iron. Iron's melting point is 2800°F (1538°C). That's about 31 times hotter than a 90°F (32°C) summer day! Tugged by gravity and being somewhat on the heavy side as metals go, the iron, a bit of nickel, and a small amount of a few other metals sank down to the center of Earth. In all, nearly one-third of young Earth's mass made its way to the planet's center. This heavy-metal slurry pushed most of the lighter elements such as oxygen and silicon out of the way, and they floated up toward Earth's outer edge. The friction from all this movement heated Earth up even more. And the heat still exists in Earth's core today. Let's take a look at Earth's layers, from the inside out.

# APPLE VS. EARTH

**AS ODD AS IT MAY SEEM,** all we need is an apple to see how Earth's layers are proportioned (see page 16 for a diagram of Earth's layers). The seeds in the apple's center represent the solid inner core of Earth. The inner core is about 760 miles (1,220 km) thick. (Use your imagination here! While the apple has two seeds, Earth has only one inner core.) The apple's core can be compared to Earth's liquid outer core, which is 1,400 miles (2,250 km) thick. The fleshy part of the apple is its softest and largest part, much like the 1,800-mile (2,900-km)-thick semisolid and solid mantle is to Earth. And the thin skin of the apple can be compared to Earth's thin, rocky, brittle crust, which reaches only 47 miles (75 km) at its thickest.

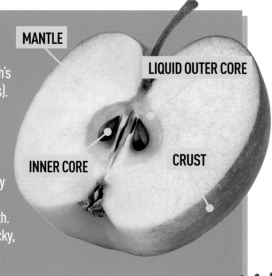

MANTLE

LIQUID OUTER CORE

INNER CORE

CRUST

**MAGNETITE IS A MINERAL** found in many different types of rocks. It's mostly gray or black, but it hides a fun surprise. As you might guess from its name, magnetite is naturally attracted to magnets. But only one type of magnetite, called lodestone, is actually magnetized, or has magnetic properties. A sort of super magnetite, lodestone is one of only two naturally magnetized minerals that exist (the other being pyrrhotite, which has very weak magnetized properties). It attracts objects such as iron and was the first natural compass ever used because it aligns with Earth's magnetic field. Scientists study magnetite to learn about how Earth's magnetic field has changed throughout history.

It's not hard to find magnetite. If you've ever seen black sand, you've seen magnetite. But if you can't tell if the beach sand between your toes contains particles of magnetite, just drag a magnet through the sand. It will pick up the magnetite instantly.

Believe it or not, some animals such as pigeons and whales have bits of magnetite in their brains, and bees have magnetite in their abdomens. The magnetite helps these animals know which direction to travel by orienting them to Earth's magnetic field, much like a compass does.

BLACK SAND IS ACTUALLY MAGNETITE. TRY DRAGGING A MAGNET THROUGH IT.

## Earth's Layers From the Inside Out

By about four billion years ago, fewer and fewer space rocks were bumping into Earth. Without these crashing forces, Earth began to cool. That magma ocean that had been roiling and bubbling and spewing slowly cooled to form the three main layers of Earth: the crust, mantle, and core.

The uppermost rocky crust is the layer of Earth that supports life. The mantle is the middle layer and is divided into the upper and lower mantle. The rocky upper mantle lithosphere is further divided into the lithosphere and asthenosphere. The slow-moving lower mantle shapes Earth into mountains and valleys and continents with the help of moving plates, or slabs, of Earth. The core, which is divided into the liquid outer core and the solid inner core, rounds out the three layers.

Let's take a closer look at each of these layers one at a time from the inside out.

THE HOBA METEORITE, WHICH LANDED IN NAMIBIA, AFRICA, IS MADE OF A MIX OF IRON AND NICKEL, WHICH CLOSELY RESEMBLES THE MAKEUP OF EARTH'S CORE.

## The Solid Core

Earth's inner core is a burning-hot 9000°F to 13,000°F (5000°C to 7200°C). That's hotter than the sun's surface and certainly hot enough to melt iron and nickel, the core's main ingredients. But Earth's weight puts so much pressure on the inner core that it squeezes the iron and nickel until they become solid.

Surrounding the inner core is the outer core, a liquid concoction that's also mostly made of iron and nickel. The liquid state of the outer core helps create Earth's magnetic field. It's this magnetic field that makes your compass point to the north. The magnetic field extends from Earth's outer core into space and protects Earth from the damaging effects of the solar wind by deflecting it away. Remember the solar wind? It's what blew debris through space, which resulted in the formation of the gas giant planets.

EARTH'S MAGNETIC FIELD MAKES YOUR COMPASS POINT NORTH.

## The Magnificent Mantle

Beyond Earth's core is the rocky realm of the mantle, Earth's largest layer, filling up 84 percent of the planet by volume. The mantle is made of rock called silicates, such as olivine and garnet. Like the core, the mantle is divided into two main regions, the lower mantle and the upper mantle.

The lower mantle is solid rock and reaches a temperature of 6692°F to 9400°F (3700°C to 5200°C). It's hot enough in the lower mantle to partially melt rock, but, as with the inner core, the pressure is so great that the rock is forced into a solid. Over millions of years, though, the rock slowly moves and convects, which means that the hotter rock rises and the colder rock sinks.

In the transition zone between the upper and lower mantle, the rock gets denser (compact and heavy). This zone also holds a surprise—water—although it's in a very

OLIVINE, ALSO FOUND IN EARTH'S MANTLE, MAKES THIS SAND GREEN!

GREEN SAND ON SOUTH POINT BEACH IN HAWAII, U.S.A.

# LAYER STATS

| LAYER | TEMPERATURE RANGE | DEPTH RANGE | CONSISTENCY | COMPOSITION |
|---|---|---|---|---|
| CRUST | 32°F–1472°F (0°C–800°C) | Oceanic crust: 0–6.2 miles (0–10 km) Continental crust: 18.5–50 miles (30-80 km) | Solid | Oceanic crust: Plagioclase and pyroxene rock Continental crust: Feldspar and quartz-based rock |
| UPPER MANTLE (Asthenosphere and Mantle Lithosphere) | 1472°F–2732°F (800°C–1500°C) | 50–255 miles (80–410 km) | Solid | Peridotites and eclogites |
| TRANSITION ZONE | 2732°F–3092°F (1500°C–1700°C) | 255–410 miles (410–660 km) | Solid | Peridotites |
| LOWER MANTLE | 3092°F–5252°F (1700°C–2900°C) | 311–1,802 miles (500–2,900 km) | Solid | Rock made of iron and magnesium silicate minerals |
| OUTER CORE | 5252°F–7232°F (2900°C–4000°C) | 1,802–3,200 miles (2,900–5,150 km) | Liquid | Iron, nickel, sulfur, and oxygen |
| INNER CORE | 7232°F–14,432°F (4000°C–8000°C) | 3,300-3,959 miles (5,151-6,371 km) | Solid | Iron and nickel |

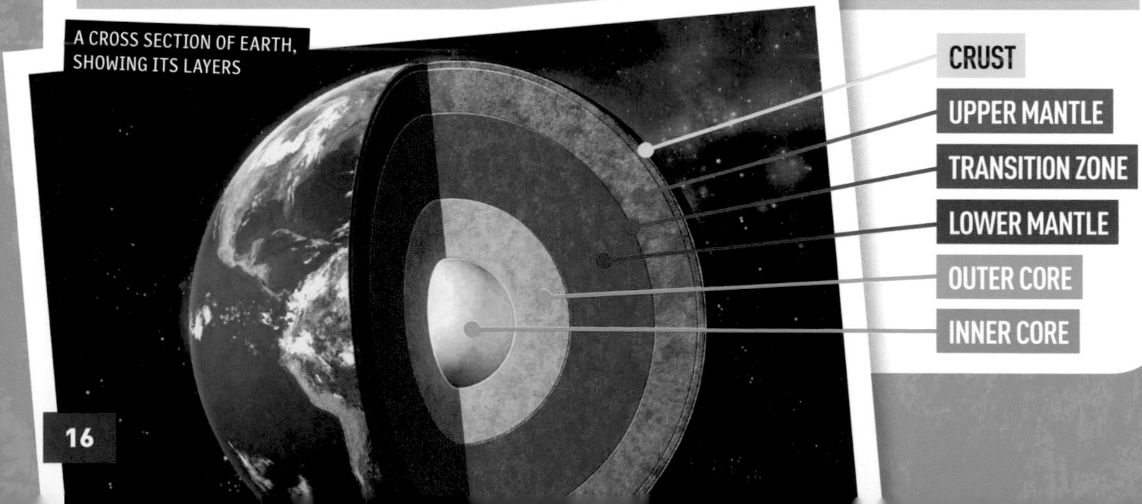

A CROSS SECTION OF EARTH, SHOWING ITS LAYERS

CRUST

UPPER MANTLE

TRANSITION ZONE

LOWER MANTLE

OUTER CORE

INNER CORE

# RIDING THE WAVES

**WE KNOW A LOT ABOUT THE INNER WORKINGS OF EARTH,** but no one has been able to explore past Earth's crust. That's right. We have never broken through the top one percent of Earth. How, then, do we know so much about Earth's layers? The answer is earthquakes!

Earthquakes can occur as deep as 435 miles (700 km). They create seismic waves, or vibrations, that scientists analyze to help them get a glimpse of Earth's interior. Seismic waves catapult through Earth in all directions away from an earthquake's origin, or center. The length and speed of these waves change depending on the material in their path. P-waves are fast and can travel through both rock and water. S-waves are slower and can't travel through water. Scientists study the changes in seismic wave speed to get a good idea of what's within and below the crust.

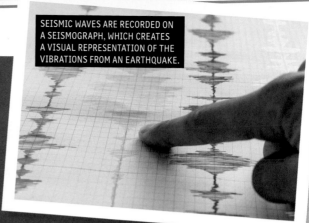

SEISMIC WAVES ARE RECORDED ON A SEISMOGRAPH, WHICH CREATES A VISUAL REPRESENTATION OF THE VIBRATIONS FROM AN EARTHQUAKE.

different form than we're familiar with. Instead of being a liquid, the water is in the form of molecules found in crystals. A molecule is the smallest part of a substance that has all of the substance's characteristics. Rock crystals in the transition zone hold as many water molecules as Earth's oceans! Beyond the transition zone is the upper mantle. The upper mantle is further divided into two layers: the asthenosphere and the mantle lithosphere.

The asthenosphere is made up of a relatively weak layer of dense rock. The pressure and heat in the asthenosphere is high enough to partially melt this rock into a consistency that might remind you of thick peanut butter. This partly molten rock can move slowly, and it allows the lithosphere above it to move. The pressure at the top of the asthenosphere isn't as strong as it is at the bottom, so small pockets of magma can form.

The lithosphere drifts and slides on top of the asthenosphere. It includes the uppermost part of the upper mantle, called the mantle lithosphere, and the crust. The upper mantle is brittle rather than gooey, and Earth's crust is made up of solid rock and minerals. A lot of activity takes place within the lithosphere, and that activity slowly changes the face of Earth. It shapes new mountains, creates ocean basins, and spreads continents apart to form great rift valleys that are deep and narrow.

THE DARVAZA GAS CRATER IN TURKMENISTAN

## Crust

The journey through Earth has taken us 3,959 miles (6,371 km) from our planet's core to its crust. The rocky crust is the layer of Earth we're most

# THE PANGAEA PUZZLE

**IN THE EARLY 1900s,** some scientists noticed that fossils of the same kinds of extinct animals were being found on various continents. This had them scratching their heads. It seemed impossible for these animals to have crossed vast seas to get from one continent to another ... unless at one time very long ago, the continents had been connected. This seemed the likeliest possibility, but no one at that time knew how one huge landmass could break apart and form the modern-day continents. In the following decades, many scientists put their heads together, and the theory of plate tectonics and its role in moving continents came to light.

German scientist Alfred Wegener is considered the father of plate tectonics. He's the one who developed the theory that one huge supercontinent he named Pangaea had separated and drifted apart, becoming the continents we have today.

THE SUPERCONTINENT PANGAEA, 270 MILLION YEARS AGO

FOUR OF THE SEVEN CONTINENTS AS WE KNOW THEM TODAY

familiar with because it's just beneath the ground we walk on. But even though the crust is part of our everyday lives, it's still full of surprises.

When we're digging in the sand or planting a tree, the crust seems quite thick. But it's really the thinnest of Earth's layers. The crust makes up only one percent of Earth, and it comes in two varieties: the continental crust and the oceanic crust. The continental crust is made mostly of hard feldspar and quartz-based rock, and the oceanic crust is made mostly of hard plagioclase and pyroxene rock. Continental crust is the solid land beneath our feet and is generally older, thicker, and less dense than oceanic crust, which is the foundation for the ocean floor.

## Earth on the Move

You can't feel it, but as part of the lithosphere, Earth's crust is constantly moving. You aren't aware of this because most of Earth's movements are too slow for you to feel. And much of the crust's activity is caused by what's going on underneath it.

Currents in the lithosphere are the sources of this activity. The currents cause slabs of dense oceanic lithosphere to move underneath the less dense continental lithosphere. This is called subduction. Sudden subduction can cause an earthquake.

The mantle's currents aren't like the water currents in an ocean, which are caused by winds, temperature, and other factors. Instead, the mantle's currents are created by an interaction of cooling and warming magma called convection. Hot magma is carried by these currents up to the lithosphere as cooler, heavier material flows downward toward Earth's core. You can see how this cycle of movement works at a much faster pace by watching the bubbles in boiling water.

MOUNT EVEREST IS THE **HIGHEST** MOUNTAIN IN THE WORLD, BUT IT USED TO BE PART OF THE OCEAN FLOOR!

EARTH'S CRASHING PLATES PUSHED MOUNT EVEREST TO ITS MOUNTAINOUS HEIGHT OF 29,035 FEET (8,850 M) ABOVE SEA LEVEL. CLIMBERS WHO HAVE MADE IT TO THE PEAK HAVE FOUND ANCIENT SHELLS PRESSED INTO THE ROCK.

Over time, the force from currents in the mantle, and possibly meteorite impacts billions of years ago, have broken the crust into about 15 large pieces of lithosphere that we call tectonic plates. Seven of these plates reflect the continents (and ocean) that they support. They are the African, Antarctic, Eurasian, Australian, North American, Pacific, and South American plates.

These huge plates ride atop the molten rock of the asthenosphere. But it's not like riding a wave or a roller coaster or going on a boat ride. The movement is slow. The plates move at about the same speed as the growth of your hair. That's about four to six inches (10 to 15 cm) a year. Sometimes, though, the action gets faster and stronger. That's when you can

THINGVELLIR NATIONAL PARK, ICELAND, IS WHERE THE NORTH AMERICAN AND EURASIAN TECTONIC PLATES MEET.

actually feel Earth move. That's what can cause an earthquake.

As they float on the asthenosphere, tectonic plates can bump into one another or grind and scrape against each other. One plate slipping past or under another may create a sudden surge of jerks and jolts that can shake the earth for miles (km) around. They can shake you, too, if the earthquake is strong enough. Sometimes plates crash into each other with such force that they push up the crust, gradually forming mountains and valleys.

You may also feel Earth move during a dramatic volcanic explosion of fire and ash and rock and lava. But how does lava leak out of Earth, and what impact do volcanoes have on Earth's crust? Let's take a look behind the scenes to find out.

## Under Pressure

When we think of a volcano, most of us come up with an image of a mountain blasting its lid off, spewing lava in all directions. But a volcano really begins as a tear in Earth's crust that allows small pockets of magma to escape. Pathways to Earth's crust have already been carved out between the moving tectonic plates, and that's often the route magma takes before it explodes onto Earth's surface as lava. Sometimes the magma flows out; sometimes it explodes with great force, spitting ash, rocks, and lava high into the air. Heat and pressure are what drive the explosion.

Magma is mostly molten rock, but gas and water are often included in the mix. The movement of convection carries the red-hot magma upward. When it reaches the cool crust, the gas and water suddenly expand and erupt in a volcanic explosion.

A volcano's violent, fiery explosions can create a lot of damage on land. People and animals may die, ash pollutes the air, and lava flows can burn and smother plants. But eventually, lava adds a lot of nutrients to the soil, which help plants grow, and lava itself builds up Earth's landscape.

Earth's formation, with its layers, magma, lava, tectonic plates, earthquakes, and volcanoes, helps introduce us to the world of rocks and minerals.

MAGMA ESCAPING THROUGH EARTH'S CORE AND BECOMING LAVA AS IT REACHES EARTH'S SURFACE

# FASCINATING VOLCANO FACTS

- The word "volcano" comes from the name Vulcan, the Roman god of fire.
- Volcanoes form on the ocean floor as well as on land. Scientists estimate that there are more than one million underwater volcanoes, although they are not all active.
- Ninety percent of Earth's volcanoes can be found in a horseshoe-shaped area of the Pacific Ocean called the Ring of Fire.
- Pumice is a volcanic rock that floats.
- There are roughly 1,900 volcanoes on Earth that are active, which means they'll probably explode again!

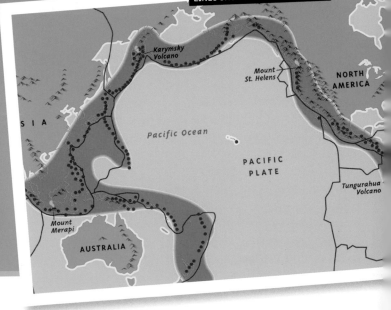

THE RING OF FIRE, SHOWN HERE IN ORANGE. RED DOTS REPRESENT VOLCANOES, AND THE PURPLE LINES SHOW PLATE BOUNDARIES.

Karymsky Volcano

Mount St. Helens

NORTH AMERICA

Pacific Ocean

PACIFIC PLATE

Tungurahua Volcano

Mount Merapi

AUSTRALIA

SIA

# VOLCANO VARIETIES

**ALL SORTS OF VOLCANOES DOT EARTH,** and they don't all behave in the same way or spew out the same stuff. Here are the four classifications of volcanoes:

**CINDER CONES:** Hundreds of cinder cone volcanoes have formed on Mauna Kea in Hawaii, U.S.A. These are the volcanoes you may imagine when you hear the word "volcano." They are shaped like a cone and topped with a bowl-shaped crater. Cinder cones are on the small side as far as volcanoes go. They eject fiery sprays of gas-filled lava that cool quickly in the air and fall to the ground in the form of ashes.

CINDER CONE VOLCANO: MAUNA KEA, HAWAII, U.S.A.

**COMPOSITE VOLCANOES:** Japan's Mount Fuji and Washington's Mount Rainier and Mount St. Helens are all examples of composite volcanoes. They can be large and steep-sided, and they can have several vents that are capable of producing violent eruptions. Composite volcanoes are formed by layers of lava building up over hundreds of years.

COMPOSITE VOLCANO: MOUNT FUJI, JAPAN

**LAVA DOMES:** These quieter volcanoes usually don't have enough gas and aren't under enough pressure to produce an impressive eruption. The thick lava they burp out can't flow far and instead hardens around the lava dome's vent. Some lava domes can form within other volcanoes, such as the two lava domes in Mount St. Helens. The Puy de Dôme volcanoes in France were created by an eruption more than 10,000 years ago.

LAVA DOME: PUY DE DÔME, FRANCE

**SHIELD VOLCANOES:** Mauna Loa and Kilauea of Hawaii are well-known shield volcanoes. These are wide, shallow volcanoes that often erupt quietly. The lava is mainly melted basalt, which flows so quickly that it spreads before it can build up into a steep mountain. The result is a shield-shaped volcano.

SHIELD VOLCANO: KILAUEA IN HAWAII, U.S.A. PICTURED HERE IS THE PUU OO CRATER LAKE FILLED WITH MOLTEN LAVA.

SKYSCRAPERS LIKE THESE IN NEW YORK CITY COULDN'T EXIST WITHOUT MINERALS. IRON, COPPER, AND EVEN GOLD ARE IMPORTANT IN CONSTRUCTION.

THE MANHATTAN SKYLINE IN NEW YORK CITY

## What Is a Mineral?

Minerals were around long before life existed. They are naturally made, often by cooling lava or evaporating ocean water. They are inorganic, which means they are not living or made by a living being. And most minerals are solid at room temperature.

Minerals form deep inside Earth from heat and pressure and are found all over our planet. Look around you. If you're outside, the sand and the soil and the rocks that you see are made of minerals. So are the cars and the buildings and the playground equipment. If you're inside, much of your food, your medicines, and even your countertops are likely made of minerals.

Minerals are made of atoms, the smallest possible amount of a substance. An element is made of one type of atom. The elements in minerals usually form a type of crystal that's unique to that mineral. A mineral's elements and how its crystals are arranged determine what the mineral looks like. For example, salt is a mineral with cube-shaped crystals. Look at a grain of salt under a magnifying glass, and you'll see it's a cube. More than 5,000 minerals have been discovered on Earth, and more are being found all the time.

When you look at a mineral, let's say a piece of quartz, you might think that it looks an awful lot like a rock. So what *is* the difference between a mineral and a rock? You're about to find out!

IF YOU MAGNIFY SALT, YOU'LL SEE THAT ITS CRYSTALS ARE CUBE-SHAPED.

BAKED POOP!

## FROM POOP TO MINERAL

**SUBSTANCES THAT WOULD NORMALLY NEVER MIX** may encounter one another by chance through human activity. Maybe the oddest example of this is tinnuncu-lite. This mineral was named after a bird known as the European kestrel *(Falco tinnunculus)* that pooped around a burning coal mine in Russia. When the hot gases from the mine baked the kestrel poop, tinnunculite came to be. Its status as a mineral became official in 2016.

A KESTREL IS A TYPE OF FALCON.

HOT GASES FROM A BURNING COAL MINE TURNED KESTREL POOP INTO THE MINERAL TINNUNCULITE.

## What Is a Rock?

You climb on them, you skip them, maybe you even collect them; rocks are all around you. Rocks can sparkle, or they can be dull. They can be rough or smooth. They can be decorated in stripes or in flecks. They can be soft and crumble, or they can be hard and solid. Rocks come in brown, gray, black—yellow, blue, red, pink, and, yes, purple! But what exactly is a rock?

A rock is solid (not liquid or gas) and natural (not made by people), and it's made of one or more minerals. Some rocks are organic—formed by living things. The minerals in rocks give scientists clues about Earth's history and how a rock was formed. Even if a rock is found in the desert, its minerals may tell the story of it having once been near a lake or even in an ocean. Maybe long ago it was shot out of a volcano. Scientists use minerals' clues to group the rock into one of three categories: igneous, sedimentary, or metamorphic.

## Igneous Rock

Igneous rocks come from the cooling of fiery-hot magma and lava. *Ignis* is the Latin word for fire, which is also where the word "ignite" comes from. In some cases, rocks are formed beneath Earth's surface as magma cools underground. The magma comes from small pockets of melted rock at the boundary between the lithosphere and asthenosphere. The rock forms in the crust and the mantle lithosphere. This type of igneous rock is called intrusive because the magma intrudes or flows underground. Intrusive rocks cool slowly, which allows the crystals to grow larger than those of rocks that form on Earth's surface. Granite is an example of an intrusive rock. Igneous rocks that are catapulted out of the ground with the force of a volcanic eruption are called extrusive rocks. They usually harden quickly as they flow onto Earth's cool surface. The faster cooling means smaller crystals. Basalt is an example of an extrusive igneous rock.

THE IGNEOUS ROCK FORMATIONS CALLED THE CATHEDRAL SPIRES AT CUSTER STATE PARK IN SOUTH DAKOTA, U.S.A.

SEDIMENTARY ROCK CAN SOMETIMES HOLD FOSSILIZED TREASURES, SUCH AS THIS ANCIENT SEA STAR AND TRILOBITE.

METAMORPHIC ROCK IS ROCK THAT'S BEEN TRANSFORMED— SUCH AS THIS MARBLE, WHICH USED TO BE LIMESTONE.

## Sedimentary Rock

Sedimentary rock is made up of bits and pieces of other rocks on Earth's crust. Rain, wind, ice, and even the things you do like mountain biking, off-roading, and hiking can wear away existing rock into crumbs called sediment. After being washed or blown away, a layer of sediment settles, often at the bottom of a lake. As time goes by, other layers of sediment settle on top of the first layer. Eventually, the upper layers weigh down the lower layers. The pressure becomes so strong that the pressed layers stick to one another and form sedimentary rock.

You can see the layers in sedimentary rock, and sometimes surprises hide within these layers. Plants and animals, parts of plants and animals, and impressions of plants and animals can get trapped within the layers of sediment. They get pressed and harden just like the sediment does (see chapter 3), and over millions of years, fossils are formed.

## Metamorphic Rock

The description "metamorphic" means "to change form," and that's exactly how metamorphic rock is made.

Unlike sedimentary rock, metamorphic rock forms deep underground, where temperatures are high and pressures are great. Heat and pressure can cause elements to rearrange themselves and form different minerals.

This transformation changes the existing rock, which could be igneous, sedimentary, or metamorphic, into a new and different rock.

A good example is limestone, which is a sedimentary rock. When put under high pressure and heat underground, limestone changes to the metamorphic rock marble.

UNLIKE MOST MINERALS, MERCURY IS LIQUID AT ROOM TEMPERATURE.

# MINERAL ODDITIES

**SOME MINERALS DON'T HAVE ALL THE CHARACTERISTICS OF A TYPICAL MINERAL.** One defining property of a mineral is that it's solid at room temperature. But mercury and naturally occurring ice are considered minerals even though they're liquid at room temperature.

ICE IS ANOTHER OUT-OF-THE-BOX MINERAL THAT'S LIQUID AT ROOM TEMPERATURE.

# ROCK ODDITIES

**SOMETIMES SCIENCE IS NOT EXACT.** A rock is defined as being made of minerals. But coal, obsidian, and amber are exceptions. All three are categorized as rocks, and all three lack minerals. Coal is organic, being formed by prehistoric plants and animals that have been pressed by a buildup of mud and debris and baked for millions of years. It's the only rock that burns. Obsidian is spewed from a volcano, and it cools so quickly that crystals don't have time to form. It's often described as having a glassy surface. Like coal, amber is organic. It was formed by ancient tree sap that hardened over time. Plants and insects have become trapped in amber, which has preserved their forms for millions of years.

COAL IS A ROCK, BUT NOT A MINERAL, BECAUSE IT'S MADE FROM ORGANIC MATERIAL.

OBSIDIAN, OR VOLCANIC GLASS, COOLS SO FAST THAT IT HAS NO CRYSTALS.

HERE'S A STICKY ONE! AMBER WAS ONCE TREE SAP THAT HARDENED OVER MILLIONS OF YEARS.

# THE ROCK CYCLE

## 2. IGNEOUS ROCK
SOME OF THE MAGMA HARDENS INTO IGNEOUS ROCKS, SUCH AS GRANITE OR DIORITE. THE MAGMA THAT DOESN'T REMAIN IN PLACE RISES TO EARTH'S SURFACE. THERE, IT CAN ERUPT AS LAVA. AS THE LAVA COOLS, IT HARDENS INTO IGNEOUS VOLCANIC ROCK SUCH AS BASALT.

COOLING

MELTING

HEAT AND PRESSURE

## 1. MAGMA
DEEP UNDERGROUND, METAMORPHIC ROCKS MELT TO FORM MAGMA.

WEATHERING AND EROSION

## 3. SEDIMENTS
ROCKS ON EARTH'S SURFACE ARE BATTERED BY RAIN, WIND, AND ICE IN A PROCESS CALLED WEATHERING. OVER TIME, WEATHERING BREAKS THE ROCKS INTO SMALL PARTICLES. EVENTUALLY, THE PARTICLES ARE DEPOSITED AS SEDIMENTS INTO STREAMS, LAKES, AND OCEANS.

MELTING

COMPACTION AND CEMENTATION

## 5. METAMORPHIC ROCK
THE UPPER PORTION OF EARTH'S MANTLE AND CRUST IS BROKEN UP INTO TECTONIC PLATES. SOME PLATES SPREAD APART AND RELEASE MAGMA, WHILE OTHERS COLLIDE. WHEN THIS HAPPENS, ROCKS ON THE SURFACE CAN BE PUSHED UNDER THE SURFACE, WHERE THEY ARE HEATED AND/OR SQUEEZED. EVENTUALLY, THEY FORM METAMORPHIC ROCKS.

WEATHERING AND EROSION

WEATHERING AND EROSION

HEAT AND PRESSURE

## 4. SEDIMENTARY ROCK
THE SEDIMENTS ARE SQUEEZED AND CEMENTED TOGETHER TO FORM SEDIMENTARY ROCK. OVER TIME, IT WEATHERS AND RETURNS TO SEDIMENT OR IS DRIVEN BACK UNDER EARTH'S SURFACE THROUGH TECTONIC PLATES.

## The Rock Cycle

Even though rocks are solid and hard, they go through many transformations over time. Rocks can melt, get squashed, and even vaporize. And new rock is being formed all the time on and in Earth, even right at this moment.

The rock cycle illustrates the changes rocks go through and explains how the three types of rock are related to one another. The formation of rocks and the changes rocks go through don't happen quickly, though. They happen on the geologic time clock, which means the changes take many thousands of years. And since this is a cycle, the changes never stop.

But what do you think is the driving force behind the rock cycle? If you guessed plate tectonics, then you guessed right.

## Plate Tectonics

The rock on Earth's surface can be weathered by such forces as wind, rain, ice, and changes in temperatures. No rock is too hard for this whittling away of stone. Then erosion through winds, flowing rivers, rainfall, glaciers, and gravity whisks the sediment to low-lying areas, such as lake beds, ocean floors, or deserts. And after thousands of years, the sediment of rock and other debris is transformed into sedimentary

A SCUBA DIVER SWIMS THROUGH NESGJA, A SMALL FISSURE IN NORTH ICELAND.

rock. Here's where tectonic plates come into play.

Piping-hot magma can break through to Earth's surface on land or on the ocean floor after an earthquake releases pressure on a fault. A fault is a break in Earth's crust. Sudden movement of the crust on each side of the fault releases pressure and causes an earthquake. The magma rises up along the fault at what are called divergent boundaries, areas where tectonic plates move away from each other. This magma cools into intrusive igneous rock, or it flows onto the surface and forms extrusive igneous rocks, such as basalt. At convergent boundaries, areas where one tectonic plate forces another beneath it, the cooler, denser, and heavier igneous, sedimentary, or metamorphic rock sinks back into Earth's mantle to be pressed, heated, and formed into metamorphic rock. Earthquakes, volcanoes, and plate collisions that form mountains bring metamorphic rock to Earth's surface in a process called uplift.

Now you have a good idea of what rocks and minerals are and what the forces are that bring them to Earth's surface. It's time to grab your magnifying glasses, because we're going to take a much closer look at the colorful and fascinating world of minerals and rocks.

# PLATE BOUNDARIES

**SCIENTISTS HAVE COME UP WITH A THEORY** about Earth's 15 lithosphere plates and how they move. Part of this theory of plate tectonics is that the plates interact with one another in different ways depending on their boundaries, or edges. At transform boundaries, one plate slides past another. At convergent boundaries, one plate collides with another, forcing one of the plates to slide underneath the other. Plates move away from each other at divergent boundaries. Magma from the mantle can bubble up at divergent boundaries on the ocean floor and form underwater mountain ranges.

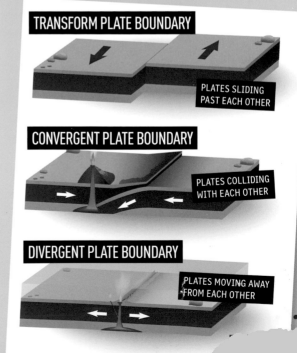

TRANSFORM PLATE BOUNDARY

PLATES SLIDING PAST EACH OTHER

CONVERGENT PLATE BOUNDARY

PLATES COLLIDING WITH EACH OTHER

DIVERGENT PLATE BOUNDARY

PLATES MOVING AWAY FROM EACH OTHER

# ROCK OUT!

## MAKE YOUR OWN VOLCANO

**Here's a fun "exploding" experiment.** You can follow this recipe and add your own creative touches with paint and decorations. Add glitter or some tonic water with quinine. Quinine has properties that will glow when you shine a black light on it. Give your clay and paint enough time to dry.

## What to do:

1. Line a cookie sheet with wax paper or foil, then place your container in the center of the cookie sheet.

2. Mold your clay into the shape of a volcano around the container. Make sure the clay wraps snugly around the mouth of the container. If you want, decorate your volcano with plastic plants, animals, houses—get creative! Let the clay dry.

3. Paint the volcano, and let the paint dry.

4. Mix the baking soda, dish soap, and food coloring in a cup or bowl, and then pour it into the container. Use a funnel if necessary.

5. Make sure everyone is ready to be wowed, and then pour in the vinegar and watch the eruption!

POUR IN THE VINEGAR AND GET READY FOR THE ERUPTION!

# For this activity, you'll need:

1 COOKIE SHEET

WAX PAPER OR ALUMINUM FOIL

PAINTS AND PAINT BRUSHES

PLASTIC PLANTS, ANIMALS, HOUSES (OPTIONAL)

CLAY

1 EMPTY CONTAINER, SUCH AS A JAR, SODA CAN, OR PLASTIC BOTTLE

2 TBSP (30 ML) LIQUID DISH SOAP

½ CUP (118 ML) WHITE VINEGAR

WHITE VINEGAR

2 TO 3 TBSP (29 TO 43 G) BAKING SODA

Pure
Baking Soda

Baking Soda

Easy Open Package

Household Uses
Fresh Box

Net WT 17.5 OZ (1000gr)

A CUP OR BOWL

6 TO 7 DROPS RED FOOD COLORING

FUNNEL (OPTIONAL)

AGATES, SUCH AS THIS BLUE ONE, FORM IN POCKETS OR CRACKS OF OTHER ROCKS.

# CHAPTER 2

# A KALEIDOSCOPE OF CRYSTALS AND MINERALS

## MADAGASCAR IS THE FOURTH BIGGEST ISLAND IN THE WORLD.

Off the southeast corner of Africa, this island is full of geologic activity, including frequent small earthquakes. And there's evidence that the island is breaking apart.

DR. SARAH STAMPS

To find out if the island really is splitting apart because of Earth's movements, I've been going there with a team to measure the different movements between northern and southern Madagascar, and the different movements between eastern and western Madagascar.

With our instruments, we try to measure these movements down to a tiny fraction of an inch.

One of the places we visit year after year to make measurements is in a rain forest. And in that rain forest, there happens to be a mine. But it's not what you would typically think of as a mine.

This mine is just a person using tools to chip away at rock. It's a very slow way to mine. He can use fire to help break up the rock and make it weaker along fracture points. But mostly, he works on the rocks with his hands until he physically carves them out of the earth. It's really incredible.

This person, the miner, was working near a cliff very close to our instruments, and his mining would cause something completely unexpected.

Every time we take measurements, we add benchmarks to help us with our research. A benchmark is a small steel pin that is about the size of a dime in diameter and a few inches in length.

To install a benchmark, we drill several inches into rock and use epoxy to glue the benchmark there, so it is fixed securely to the rock and we don't have to worry about it coming loose.

Every time we go back to the site, we measure the same benchmark. We can detect if the benchmark has moved even just a tiny bit with our GPS equipment.

We had already measured this place twice and were returning to measure it a third time. But when we got there, we were in for a surprise.

Due to weathering and mining, the cliff had fallen totally off! Luckily our equipment hadn't fallen, but our benchmark was gone! And with that benchmark went some of our data from our fieldwork.

Although we get a lot of our natural resources, such as iron and copper, from mines, mining does do damage to Earth—and sometimes to scientific fieldwork.

DR. STAMPS SETS UP HER EQUIPMENT IN MADAGASCAR.

DR. STAMPS'S PRECISE INSTRUMENTS CAN MEASURE GEOLOGIC ACTIVITY DOWN TO A TINY FRACTION OF AN INCH.

GPS EQUIPMENT THAT DR. STAMPS SET UP WITH HER TEAM ON THE COAST OF MADAGASCAR

# SALT, SNOWFLAKES, AND SOME TYPES OF BEACH SAND HAVE SOMETHING IN COMMON.

**They are all crystals. A crystal is a solid material made of atoms.**

MESOLITE HAS AN ACICULAR HABIT, WITH NEEDLELIKE CRYSTALS.

What makes a crystal's atoms special is that they are arranged in a repeating pattern inside the crystal. The pattern is called a lattice. The lattice is three-dimensional, having height, width, and depth. It is also symmetrical, so it looks exactly the same when it's flipped or turned. Each type of crystal has a different way of attaching new atoms to its lattice, repeating the pattern as a crystal grows. All the world's crystals come in seven basic lattice shapes, also called crystal systems: cubic/isometric, hexagonal, monoclinic, orthorhombic, tetragonal, triclinic, and trigonal. (See the opposite page for more on crystal systems.)

Even though they aren't alive, crystals grow. At least, that's how scientists describe how crystals form, or crystallize. Crystals grow in three types of environments: in magma, in liquid such as water, and in vapor. For example, diamond crystals grow from magma, ice crystals form as frost on windows from freezing water vapor in the air, and sodium chloride (salt) crystals form as ocean water evaporates. Crystals that cool slowly have more time to grow, so they're bigger than those that cool quickly. In Naica, Mexico, for example, 980 feet (300 m) below the desert floor, million-year-old white selenite crystals have grown to be 36 feet (11 m) long and 13 feet (4 m) wide!

The general appearance of a crystal is called its habit. A crystal's habit is often the same shape as its lattice. You can see this by looking at grains of salt under a microscope. The salt crystal has a cube-shaped lattice. As you peer into the microscope, you'll see that each salt grain is also cube-shaped—a bigger version of its lattice. Conditions such as temperature and pressure during a crystal's growth can affect its habit, causing the cool-looking variations we often see among individuals of one type of crystal. Snowflakes, for example, have sharp points when they grow in very cold temperatures. Their tips are more rounded when they grow in warmer temperatures.

Scientists have identified and named many crystal habits, but here are a few that are more common:

- Acicular: Long, needlelike crystal
- Bladed: Long, flat crystal
- Columnar: Separate, often parallel columns
- Prismatic: Long with four or more equal-size sides

# 7 CRYSTAL SYSTEMS

**ALL THE WORLD'S CRYSTALS COME IN THESE SEVEN BASIC LATTICE SHAPES,** also called crystal systems.

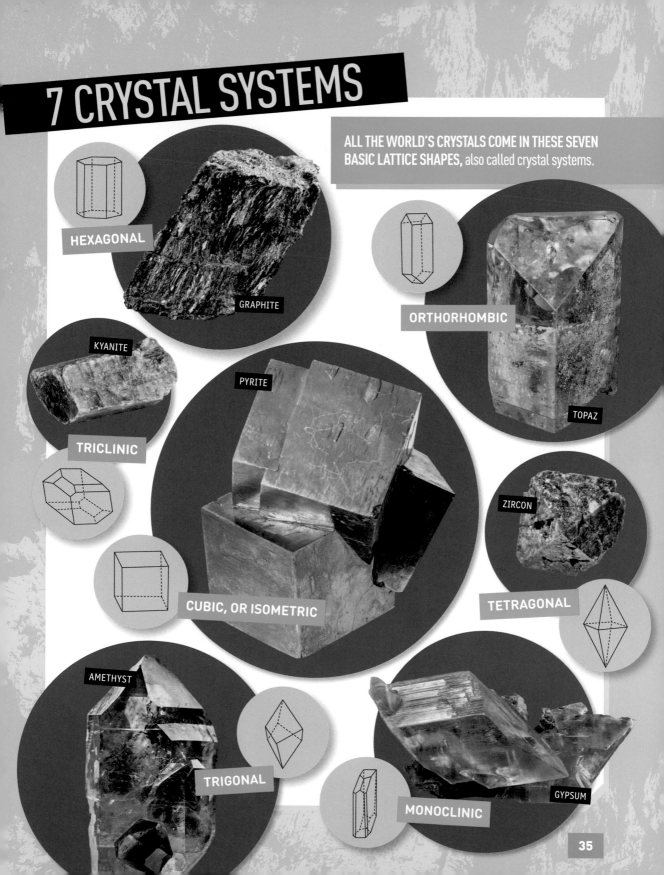

HEXAGONAL

GRAPHITE

ORTHORHOMBIC

TOPAZ

KYANITE

TRICLINIC

PYRITE

ZIRCON

CUBIC, OR ISOMETRIC

TETRAGONAL

AMETHYST

TRIGONAL

MONOCLINIC

GYPSUM

KNOWN AS THE EMPRESS OF URUGUAY, THIS HUGE GEODE IS 11 FEET TALL AND WEIGHS 2.5 TONS. THAT'S ABOUT THE WEIGHT OF A CAR!

THE EMPRESS OF URUGUAY IS ACTUALLY LOCATED IN THE CRYSTAL CAVES MUSEUM IN QUEENSLAND, AUSTRALIA.

# HIDDEN GEMS

**DID YOU KNOW THAT CRYSTALS CAN GROW INSIDE A ROCK?** How does this happen? When an igneous rock forms, a bubble of gas can get trapped inside, leaving a cavity, or hole, in the rock. Cavities can also form in sedimentary rock when minerals dissolve or organic matter decomposes. These rocks might look solid, but they have tiny pores. Water rich with dissolved minerals can seep into the rock through these pores. After the water evaporates, the minerals remain. Over thousands of years of water seeping through the rock and crystals forming, a geode forms. On the outside, geodes look as plain as any ordinary rock. But when you cut one in half, a world of sparkling crystal awaits. Quartz is the most common mineral to form in a geode.

Geodes come in all sizes. Some are small, about the size of a golf ball. Others, like the Empress of Uruguay, the largest amethyst geode, is about 11 feet (3.3 m) tall and weighs about 2.5 tons (2.3 t). But the biggest geode in the world that has been discovered so far is also a cave. Eighteen feet (5 m) across at its widest point, Crystal Cave in Ohio, U.S.A., is filled with celestite crystals, some weighing more than 300 pounds (136 kg). Over the years, the celestite crystal had been mined and used to make the color red in fireworks.

THESE ARE CELESTITE CRYSTALS, LIKE THE ONES FOUND IN CRYSTAL CAVE IN OHIO.

## From Crystal to Mineral

Trying to figure out the difference between a crystal and a mineral can get confusing. After all, crystals grow from mineral-saturated magma, liquid, and vapor, and minerals are filled with crystals. The end result is that every mineral is a crystal, and every mineral also forms a crystal.

Minerals form naturally and so do crystals. All minerals are inorganic, which means they are not alive, and they are not formed from something that was alive. But some crystals form organically from living things, so they're not minerals. Sugar is a good example of this. Sugar forms crystals, but it is not a mineral because it comes from sugarcane and from sugar beets, which are plants.

Then there are polymorphs, two or more different minerals that are made of the same crystal. The difference in the structure of a crystal's lattice can determine the type of mineral it forms. Believe it or not, graphite, the point of your pencil that rubs off on paper into letters and drawings, is made of exactly the same crystal as a diamond: carbon. How can this be? It all has to do with the amount of pressure the carbon was under as it formed and how the carbon is structured.

Carbon needs to be squeezed at a very high pressure to form a diamond, whereas lower pressure helps form graphite. The lattice, its arrangement of atoms, also determines whether you have a million-dollar diamond or a great way to take notes in school. A diamond's lattice structure is three-dimensional, with each carbon linked to four other carbons. This forms a strong bond and is a reason diamonds are so hard. Graphite's lattice structure, on the other hand, is two-dimensional, loosely layered, and made of six-sided, or hexagonal, rings of carbon that look somewhat like chicken wire. It is this weaker structure of the carbon's atoms that makes graphite soft enough to write with.

## Bold Building Blocks

Minerals are the building blocks of rocks. They're found all over the world, and we use them every day. We rub minerals such as zinc and sulfur on our skin. We drink and eat minerals such as calcium and magnesium to stay strong and healthy. Your cell phone, furniture, countertops, pencils, coins, even your toilets are made with minerals. Some minerals like platinum and gold can be worth a lot of money. With all these uses and with so much variety, how can you tell if something's a mineral?

Mineralogists are scientists who study minerals. They've come up with five characteristics that every mineral must have:

1. A mineral must be solid. That means oil, water, quicksand, or any sort of vapor or other liquid *can't* be a mineral.

2. Minerals are made up of one or more elements. You've likely heard of some of these elements. Oxygen is in the air you breathe, helium is the gas in birthday balloons that keeps them aloft, a diamond is a form of the element carbon. The combination of elements in each mineral is unique to that mineral. For example, quartz is made of one part silicon and two parts oxygen. No other

THOUGH SUGAR FORMS CRYSTALS, IT COMES FROM PLANTS, SO IT CAN'T BE A MINERAL.

mineral has that combination of elements.

3. The elements in a mineral must form a crystal.
4. All minerals must be inorganic, which means that they're not alive. So minerals are neither plant nor animal, and they can't be made by plants or animals, either. That rules out pearls, which are made by oysters, and wood, which comes from trees.
5. Natural minerals come from Earth. So-called minerals created in a laboratory are not true minerals. For example, iron is a mineral, but steel is not because it's made by people by adding a bit of carbon to the iron.

## Name That Mineral

New minerals are being discovered every day, and as of 2018, the number has risen to more than 5,000. So how are minerals identified? Can you go outside, pick one up, and know right away what type of mineral you're holding? Maybe. You might be able to recognize quartz or gold just by looking at it. But to truly identify a mineral, you need to know its chemical formula, which tells you what elements the mineral is made of and its crystal lattice. In most cases a microscope is needed to figure these things out. But you're not completely out of luck if you don't happen to have a microscope or a lab is miles away. Frequently, a mineral's characteristics give away its identity. To try to identify a mineral, you typically need to describe its color, luster, streak, cleavage, fracture, specific gravity, and hardness. These are all known together as the mineral's properties.

## Color

A mineral's color may be the easiest property to describe, but it's the least helpful when it comes to identification. That's because more than one mineral may share the same color, and some minerals come in a variety of colors depending on the other bits of elements, or impurities, they may have. For example, both gold and pyrite (also called fool's gold) are gold in color even though they're different minerals. Transparent, or see-through, minerals are more likely to have color variations than the minerals that are opaque. Quartz can be colorless, but if it has a trace amount of iron in it, then it's purple. And you can find white, brown, orange, red, gray, or pink quartz as well, depending on the other bits of elements in the quartz.

The mineral corundum is another example of how you can't rely on color alone when identifying minerals. If you find corundum with a trace amount of iron or titanium in it, you've found a blue sapphire. But if the corundum has a bit of chromium, you have a red ruby. Depending on the impurities, corundum also comes in white, yellow, green, purple, and black. Without impurities, corundum is colorless.

TO IDENTIFY A MINERAL, YOU USUALLY NEED LAB EQUIPMENT. HERE, A PERSON IS USING A DRILL.

A SAPPHIRE CRYSTAL IN THE MINERAL CORUNDUM

# FIREWORKS!

**A FOURTH OF JULY CELEBRATION** wouldn't be the same without fireworks. As you watch the dramatic explosions, do you ever wonder what these sky sparklers are made of and where those brilliant colors come from? Well, wonder no more. Minerals are responsible for these brilliant bursts of color.

It all starts with black powder, which is a mixture of potassium nitrate, charcoal, and sulfur. This powder mixture is packed into the bottom compartment of a two-compartment paper or cardboard tube called a mortar. The top compartment holds metals and minerals pressed and bound together to form pellets called stars. The way these stars are arranged within the mortar determines the firework's shape, whether it's round, star-shaped, oval, or elongated. The metals and minerals within the stars give fireworks their colors and flashes. A long fuse attached to the bottom compartment is lit, causing the entire mortar to explode into the air. Another fuse inside catches fire and ignites the bottom compartment, sprinkling the sky with an explosion of dazzling colors.

## INDIVIDUAL MINERALS AND METALS PRODUCE COLORS USED IN FIREWORKS.

**BLUES:** COPPER, MOSTLY FROM THE MINERAL CHALCOPYRITE; AZURITE; MALACHITE
**GREENS:** BARIUM, MOSTLY FROM THE MINERAL BARITE
**REDS:** STRONTIUM, MOSTLY FROM THE MINERAL CELESTITE
**YELLOWS:** SODIUM

## MINERAL AND METAL MIXTURES CREATE MORE COLORS.

**ORANGES:** STRONTIUM AND SODIUM
**PURPLES:** COPPER AND STRONTIUM
**SILVERS:** TITANIUM, ZIRCONIUM, AND MAGNESIUM

## MINERALS AND METALS CAN ALSO CREATE SPECIAL EFFECTS.

**FLASHES:** FINE ALUMINUM POWDER
**FLASHES SHOWERING DOWNWARD:** ALUMINUM FLAKES OR GRAINS
**GOLD SPARKS:** IRON FILINGS, MOSTLY FROM THE MINERAL HEMATITE, AND SMALL BITS OF CHARCOAL
**SERIES OF FLASHES:** MAGNESIUM AND ALUMINUM

# NONMETALLIC SPARKLE RATING

Luster describes how shiny something is. Minerals can be metallic—shiny, like gold—or nonmetallic. Nonmetallic sparkle covers many minerals, and there are lots of words scientists use to describe nonmetallic luster. Here are some examples. See what minerals in your collection fit these descriptions.

**ADAMANTINE:** Transparent to translucent; hard, brilliant, shiny; *Sample minerals:* Diamond, zircon

**RESINOUS:** Resinlike, honeylike; *Sample mineral:* Orpiment

**VITREOUS, GLASSY:** Looks like glass; *Sample minerals:* Quartz, pollucite

**PEARLY:** Iridescent, luster of pearls; *Sample minerals:* Stellerite, barite

**GREASY:** Looks thinly covered in oil or grease; *Sample mineral:* Nepheline

**SILKY:** Fine fiberlike structure, silk cloth; *Sample minerals:* Malachite, actinolite

**EARTHY:** Dull, rough texture; porous, or speckled with holes; *Sample minerals:* Kaolinite, anglesite

**PITCHY:** Tarlike, often radioactive; *Sample mineral:* Uraninite

**SUBVITREOUS:** Looks like a less brilliant glass; *Sample mineral:* Howlite

**WAXY:** Looks coated with wax; *Sample minerals:* Variscite, chalcedony

QUARTZ HAS A VITREOUS, OR GLASSY, LUSTER.

KAOLINITE HAS AN EARTHY LUSTER.

## Luster

The next property is its luster. Although you can use luster to help you identify a mineral, it's even less reliable than using color. That's because there's no hard-and-fast scientific method for determining luster. It's mostly left to the eye of the beholder, meaning two people can look at the same mineral and each come up with a different luster description.

You can think of luster as a mineral's sparkle rating. Luster has to do with how light reflects off a mineral's surface. An opaque mineral like silver doesn't allow light to pass through it, whereas light passes through a transparent mineral like quartz. Sometimes you can even see through a transparent mineral to the other side, as you can with ulexite.

The two main categories of luster are metallic and nonmetallic. Minerals with a metallic luster are usually opaque, and they reflect a lot of light—they're sparkly. Gold, silver, and pyrite have a metallic luster. Some minerals aren't quite as shiny, so their luster is described as being submetallic. Hematite is an example of a mineral that can have a submetallic luster. Minerals with a nonmetallic sheen come in the greatest variety of lusters, from glassy to waxy.

## Streak

The next property to look at is the color of a mineral's powder, which is called its streak. Unlike a mineral's color, which can change thanks to impurities, the streak shows a mineral's true color, and this true color doesn't change. But be aware that two different minerals that are the same color won't necessarily have streaks that are the same color. For example, real gold and fool's gold, also called pyrite, look the same. But test their streak: Real gold has a golden yellow streak, whereas fool's gold has a greenish black streak. And most light-colored nonmetallic minerals have a white or colorless streak, so determining a mineral's streak is most useful in identifying the darker-colored minerals.

It's easy to test for a mineral's streak. All you have to do is scrape it against an unglazed white piece of porcelain or ceramic tile called a streak plate. The powdery line left behind is the mineral's streak. Here are a few minerals and their streak color.

A CLOSE-UP VIEW OF BIOTITE, WHICH CLEAVES HORIZONTALLY IN ONE DIRECTION, LIKE MICA MINERALS.

- Azurite: Blue
- Cinnabar: Scarlet/brownish red
- Kyanite: Colorless
- Rutile: White, gray, or pale brown
- Zincite: Orange-yellow

## Cleavage

Cleavage is another property used to help identify a mineral. It describes one of the ways a mineral can break, or cleave. A mineral cleaves at weak points along smooth planes, or surfaces, of its crystal's lattice structure.

Remember that the crystal lattice of each type of mineral is always the same. For example, all pyrite minerals form cubic crystal lattices; all kyanite minerals form triclinic crystal lattices. So with every different lattice structure comes a different weak point, which affects how that type of mineral breaks.

Scientists use different terms to describe the common ways that minerals cleave. Basal cleavages occur horizontally in one direction and can be peeled, as with the mica minerals. Cubic cleavages form 90-degree angles and occur in three directions to form cubes, as with halite and galena. Octahedral

CUBIC CLEAVAGE

CUBIC CLEAVAGE: GALENA CLEAVES AT 90-DEGREE ANGLES TO FORM CUBES.

OCTAHEDRAL CLEAVAGE

OCTAHEDRAL CLEAVAGE: FLUORITE CLEAVES IN TRIANGULAR PLANES.

RHOMBOHEDRAL CLEAVAGE: DOLOMITE CLEAVES IN THREE DIRECTIONS, BUT NOT AT 90-DEGREE ANGLES.

RHOMBOHEDRAL CLEAVAGE

cleavages form eight triangular planes in four directions, as with fluorite. Rhombohedral cleavages form in three directions but not at 90-degree angles, as with dolomite.

Another way to measure cleavage is by what some call quality, which refers to how easily a mineral cleaves. If you collect rocks or minerals, you'll hear cleavage being referred to with words such as "perfect," "good," "imperfect," "poor," or "indistinct." Here's what they mean:

- Perfect: The mineral breaks easily, exposing a smooth, flat surface.
- Good: The mineral is harder to break, and the surface has some rough spots.
- Imperfect: The mineral is hard to break, and surfaces aren't noticeable.
- Poor: The mineral surface is rough, and edges are hard to make out.
- Indistinct: The mineral's cleavage is not noticeable.

Knowing in which directions and how easily a mineral cleaves can help identify that mineral. For example, halite, also known as rock salt, cleaves in three directions into cubes, which is the shape of its crystal lattices. Micas, on the other hand, cleave in one horizontal direction into sheets. The bonds between the sheets are weaker than those within each sheet, so micas cleave into thin layers. That's why it's easy to peel mica apart sheet by sheet.

## Fracture

Not all minerals have cleavage, but all minerals can fracture—which is another mineral property. A fracture is an irregular break in a mineral that isn't flat or smooth. Light reflects off these irregular surfaces in many directions, which makes the fractured surface look dull. Many types of minerals have characteristic fractures that help identify them. Here are some of the different types of fractures:

- Conchoidal (shelly): A fracture with a curved, smooth surface, like that of the inside of a shell, as with obsidian and quartz
- Subconchoidal: A fracture that's smooth with round corners, as with andalusite
- Earthy (crumbly): A fracture that crumbles, as with limonite
- Even (smooth): A fracture that leaves a smooth surface, as with howlite
- Uneven: A fracture that's rough, as with anhydrite and magnetite
- Hackly (jagged): A fracture with rough, sharp points, as with copper and other metals
- Splintery: A fracture that breaks in long splinters, as with fibrous minerals like kyanite

## Specific Gravity

Another way to identify a mineral is to measure how heavy and dense it is. A mineral's weight and density are together known as its specific gravity. This measurement is different from those we are familiar with, such as size and weight. Specific gravity is a ratio. It compares the density of a mineral to the density of freshwater. The specific gravity of water is 1. Anything that has a specific gravity higher than 1 is heavier than water and will sink. Anything with a specific gravity lower than 1 is lighter than water and will float.

You can get a sense of a mineral's weight just by holding it, but the only way to accurately measure a mineral's specific gravity is with

GALENA HAS A SPECIFIC GRAVITY OF 7.4 TO 7.6—A HEAVY MINERAL!

expensive equipment. Fortunately, scientists have done this and have developed handbooks and websites that list each mineral and its specific gravity, as well as other properties.

LIMONITE HAS AN EARTHY FRACTURE.

Let's say it's 1850. The gold rush is in full swing, and you've made your way to California to pan for gold. You've spent days squatting at the water's edge, finding only worthless debris. But then one day, two golden nuggets sparkle in your pan. You can't believe your eyes! You pick up both nuggets, one in each hand, and notice that although they are identical in size, one feels heavier than the other. How can that be?

If you had known about specific gravity, you'd have realized that these were two different minerals. You'd have checked a handbook or website and found out that the lightweight nugget was probably pyrite, otherwise known as fool's gold. Pyrite has a specific gravity of about 5. Gold's specific gravity is about 19. The higher the specific gravity, the heavier the mineral.

Most minerals that make up Earth's crust (such as feldspar and quartz) have a specific gravity of 2.75, which is considered average. Average specific gravity is within the range of 2.0 to 4.5. A light mineral has a specific gravity of less than 2. A specific gravity greater than 4.5 is considered heavy.

The specific gravity of a mineral can vary, and that can be blamed on impurities, or other bits of elements, in the mineral. Some specific gravity charts list a range for a mineral's specific gravity to account for this.

# Hardness

Hardness is another property that helps identify a mineral. In the mineral world, "hardness" refers to how resistant a mineral is to being scratched. Just because a mineral is hard doesn't mean that it can't be broken, though. For example, the diamond is one of the hardest minerals, but because of its perfect cleavage, it can break easily.

We have German mineralogist Friedrich Mohs to thank for having a way to describe a mineral's hardness. He created the Mohs scale of hardness to help him classify and organize a collection of minerals.

Mineralogists were already scratching minerals to identify them, so Mohs decided to perfect that method. By around 1812, he had created a way to rank mineral hardness from 1 to 10 by how easily they could be scratched.

The Mohs scale is a list of 10 common minerals called reference minerals that are rated from the softest mineral (1) to the hardest mineral (10). Any mineral can scratch all the minerals that rank lower than it.

To try to identify a mineral by its hardness, scientists figure out which of the 10 reference minerals can scratch the mineral being identified.

This test doesn't determine exactly how hard something is, but instead how hard it is in relation to the minerals on the Mohs scale. For example, if a mineral can scratch quartz but not topaz, then it's harder than quartz but not as hard as topaz. So its hardness value is 7.5 on the Mohs scale. Many people think that you can identify a diamond by seeing if it will scratch glass. Diamonds are harder than glass, so they can scratch it, but so can any other mineral that has a hardness rating greater than 6 on the Mohs scale. That's because the hardness rating for glass is 5.5.

The results of a hardness test may vary depending on which direction the scratch is made on the mineral. That's because a mineral cleaves, or breaks, at its crystal lattice's weak points. For example, the typical hardness rating of talc is 1. But if it's scratched *across* its cleavage plane, where it is stronger, rather than *along* its cleavage plane, then talc has a hardness rating that's greater than 2.

FRIEDRICH MOHS CREATED THE MOHS SCALE OF HARDNESS. MINERALOGISTS STILL USE THIS SCALE TO HELP IDENTIFY MINERALS.

IN THIS HARDNESS TEST, QUARTZ (RIGHT) SCRATCHES CALCITE (LEFT), AS YOU CAN SEE FROM THE SCRATCH MARK.

# MOHS IN THE HOUSE

**WHAT IF YOU DON'T HAPPEN TO HAVE ALL THE MOHS SCALE MINERALS** around to test your mineral for hardness? Don't worry; you're in luck. Some common household items have been ranked, so you can try to scratch them with your mineral and determine how hard it is on the Mohs scale.

A mineral is considered to be soft if it can be scratched by a fingernail. Since a fingernail is 2.5 on the Mohs hardness scale, then the mineral would rank between 1 and 2 (which scientists would write as 1-2) on the hardness scale. If it can be scratched by a knife, which is 5.5 on the scale, but not your fingernail, then the mineral is of medium hardness and ranks 3-5. A hard mineral ranks 6-9 if a knife doesn't scratch it, but it can scratch glass. Diamond is rated hardest at 10.

Fingernail: 2.5

Penny: 3

Knife blade*: 5.5

Glass: 5.5

Steel file: 6.5

Floor tile (streak plate): 6.5

*Please get permission from a grown-up before using to test hardness.

## MOHS SCALE

| MINERAL | HARDNESS |
|---------|----------|
| TALC | 1 |
| GYPSUM | 2 |
| CALCITE | 3 |
| FLUORITE | 4 |
| APATITE | 5 |
| FELDSPAR | 6 |
| QUARTZ | 7 |
| TOPAZ | 8 |
| CORUNDUM | 9 |
| DIAMOND | 10 |

# ALPHABET SOUP

**MINERALS ARE ORGANIZED BY THEIR CHEMICAL MAKEUP.** Each type of mineral has a unique chemistry that can be written as a chemical formula. A mineral's chemical makeup is what determines how it looks and all its characteristics: color, luster, streak, cleavage, fracture, specific gravity, and hardness. What goes into a chemical formula? To answer that, we have to start out very, very small.

## The Building Blocks

**AN ATOM IS A TEENY TINY PARTICLE** that is invisible to the naked eye. It is the building block of all the matter in the universe. An atom is made up of three types of particles: protons, neutrons, and electrons. The center of an atom's basic structure is called a nucleus. The nucleus is filled with protons, which have a positive charge, and neutrons, which have no charge at all. Negatively charged electrons zip around the atom's nucleus. Atoms differ based on the number of protons, electrons, and neutrons they have. And each different kind of atom makes up a different kind of element. For example, hydrogen is an element that is made up of atoms with one proton and one electron.

Atoms use their protons and electrons to bind themselves together and make molecules. Then molecules get together to form compounds and mixtures. A compound, such as water ($H_2O$) or salt (NaCl), is made of two or more elements joined together to form a separate substance. A mixture is made simply by combining two or more elements that usually can be separated again. Sea water is a mixture of salt and water.

## The Periodic Table

**ALL ELEMENTS ARE ARRANGED ON THE PERIODIC TABLE** from top to bottom, left to right, by their atomic number. An atomic number is determined by the number of protons in an atom. For instance, the element calcium has 20 protons, so its atomic number is also 20. If you change the number of protons in an atom, you change the type of element it is.

Each element is abbreviated with one or two letters on the periodic table. For example, H stands for hydrogen, O for oxygen, Fe for iron. A subscript (or small) number after an abbreviation means there are that many atoms in the molecule. If there is no number, it means there is one atom.

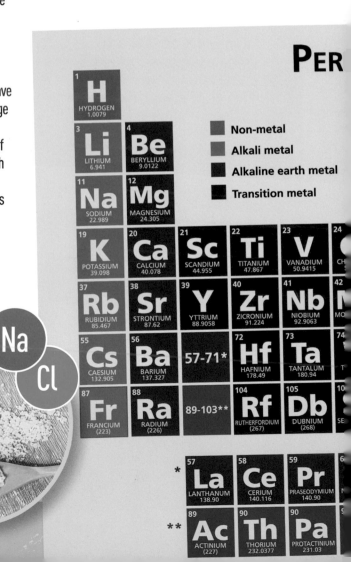

THE CHEMICAL FORMULA FOR SALT: NaCl

Na
Cl

Molecules are the smallest part of an object or substance that includes all of its properties. So you can think of atoms as the language, or the alphabet in general. Each element in the periodic table is a specific letter of the alphabet, and a molecule is a word. Let's use water as an example again. A water molecule (word) is written as $H_2O$. It has three atoms (letters) made of two elements (specific letter of the alphabet): two hydrogen atoms and one oxygen atom.

The elements are arranged on the periodic table from top to bottom and from left to right by their atomic number. The atomic number is determined by the number of protons in an element's atom and is usually represented in bold. The other number is the atom's mass, or weight. The one- and two-letter symbol represents the element's name. The two separate rows below the periodic table are drawn that way for convenience. If they were placed in their proper position, the periodic table would be too wide to read.

Chemical formulas can get more complicated as a mineral's makeup includes more elements, but this is a good beginning for understanding the basics.

THE CHEMICAL FORMULA FOR WATER: $H_2O$

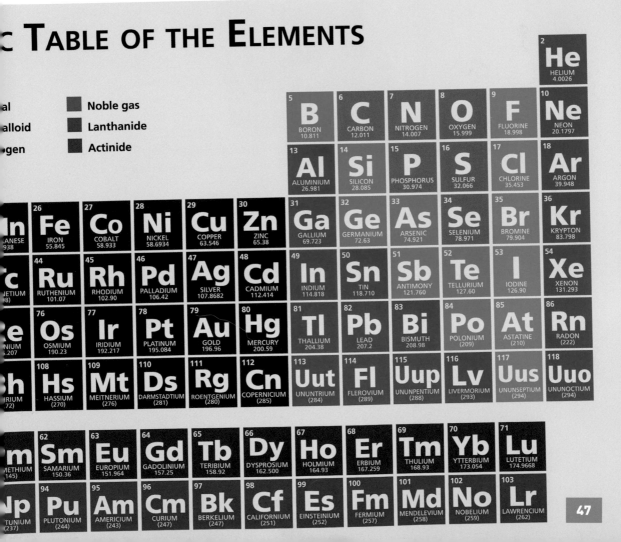

C TABLE OF THE ELEMENTS

Noble gas
Lanthanide
Actinide

| | | | | | 2 He HELIUM 4.0026 |
| 5 B BORON 10.811 | 6 C CARBON 12.011 | 7 N NITROGEN 14.007 | 8 O OXYGEN 15.999 | 9 F FLUORINE 18.998 | 10 Ne NEON 20.1797 |
| 13 Al ALUMINIUM 26.981 | 14 Si SILICON 28.085 | 15 P PHOSPHORUS 30.974 | 16 S SULFUR 32.066 | 17 Cl CHLORINE 35.453 | 18 Ar ARGON 39.948 |
| 31 Ga GALLIUM 69.723 | 32 Ge GERMANIUM 72.63 | 33 As ARSENIC 74.921 | 34 Se SELENIUM 78.971 | 35 Br BROMINE 79.904 | 36 Kr KRYPTON 83.798 |
| 49 In INDIUM 114.818 | 50 Sn TIN 118.710 | 51 Sb ANTIMONY 121.760 | 52 Te TELLURIUM 127.60 | 53 I IODINE 126.90 | 54 Xe XENON 131.293 |
| 81 Tl THALLIUM 204.38 | 82 Pb LEAD 207.2 | 83 Bi BISMUTH 208.98 | 84 Po POLONIUM (209) | 85 At ASTATINE (210) | 86 Rn RADON (222) |
| 113 Uut UNUNTRIUM (284) | 114 Fl FLEROVIUM (289) | 115 Uup UNUNPENTIUM (288) | 116 Lv LIVERMORIUM (293) | 117 Uus UNUNSEPTIUM (294) | 118 Uuo UNUNOCTIUM (294) |

| In ...ANESE ..938 | 26 Fe IRON 55.845 | 27 Co COBALT 58.933 | 28 Ni NICKEL 58.6934 | 29 Cu COPPER 63.546 | 30 Zn ZINC 65.38 |
| c ...ETIUM ..8) | 44 Ru RUTHENIUM 101.07 | 45 Rh RHODIUM 102.90 | 46 Pd PALLADIUM 106.42 | 47 Ag SILVER 107.8682 | 48 Cd CADMIUM 112.414 |
| e ...NIUM ..207 | 76 Os OSMIUM 190.23 | 77 Ir IRIDIUM 192.217 | 78 Pt PLATINUM 195.084 | 79 Au GOLD 196.96 | 80 Hg MERCURY 200.59 |
| h ...RIUM ..72) | 108 Hs HASSIUM (270) | 109 Mt MEITNERIUM (276) | 110 Ds DARMSTADTIUM (281) | 111 Rg ROENTGENIUM (280) | 112 Cn COPERNICIUM (285) |

| m ...ETHIUM (145) | 62 Sm SAMARIUM 150.36 | 63 Eu EUROPIUM 151.964 | 64 Gd GADOLINIUM 157.25 | 65 Tb TERIBIUM 158.92 | 66 Dy DYSPROSIUM 162.500 | 67 Ho HOLMIUM 164.93 | 68 Er ERBIUM 167.259 | 69 Tm THULIUM 168.93 | 70 Yb YTTERBIUM 173.054 | 71 Lu LUTETIUM 174.9668 |
| lp ...TUNIUM (237) | 94 Pu PLUTONIUM (244) | 95 Am AMERICIUM (243) | 96 Cm CURIUM (247) | 97 Bk BERKELIUM (247) | 98 Cf CALIFORNIUM (251) | 99 Es EINSTEINIUM (252) | 100 Fm FERMIUM (257) | 101 Md MENDELEVIUM (258) | 102 No NOBELIUM (259) | 103 Lr LAWRENCIUM (262) |

## Classy Minerals

We know what minerals are made of and how they can be identified. Now we need to understand how they are grouped, or classified.

The classification system most used by geologists was developed by James Dwight Dana. He was born in 1813 and became an expert on volcanoes, marine life, mountain formation, and the origin and formation of the continents. His most lasting accomplishment, though, was developing a way to organize minerals by their chemical makeup. Part of his thinking was that minerals made of similar chemicals probably developed under similar conditions of heat and pressure. They were probably found near each other as well. So he organized minerals into groups based on their chemistry, or what they were made of. Eight of the major groups are:

1. Native elements: Minerals made of only one kind of atom that are divided into metals, semimetals, and nonmetals
2. Sulfides: Minerals made of sulfur and metals
3. Oxides: Minerals made of oxygen and one or more metals
4. Carbonates: Soft minerals made of metal, carbon, and oxygen
5. Sulfates: Minerals made of metal, sulfur, and oxygen
6. Phosphates: Minerals made of phosphorous and oxygen
7. Halides: Minerals made of halogen and metals
8. Silicates: Minerals made of silicon and oxygen combined with mostly metal elements

As we explore the mineral groups, you can refer to the periodic table (see pages 46 and 47) to get a better sense of the elements that go into building minerals.

## Native Elements

We already know that minerals grow naturally and are not made in a laboratory by a person. Although some minerals can be reproduced in a laboratory, they're not considered the real deal. Most minerals are made of two or more elements. But some natural minerals are made of one element. These minerals belong to a group called native elements. Native elements vary from rare and expensive minerals, such as gold and diamonds, to widely available minerals, such as carbon and sulfur. They are divided into three groups: metals, semimetals (also called metalloids), and nonmetals.

JAMES DWIGHT DANA CLASSIFIED MINERALS' CHEMICAL FORMULAS.

### Metals

Metallic native elements are true metals: They have a shiny metal luster, are relatively heavy, and can be pounded and formed into flat, thin sheets. They also can be stretched and rolled into thin wires and can conduct electricity well. Metallic native elements include aluminum, copper, gold, lead, mercury, silver, iron, nickel, platinum, tin, and zinc. Although most metallic native elements are single-element minerals, some are made of two or more metallic elements and are known as alloys. Brass, which is a combination of copper and zinc, is an example of a native alloy.

# NATIVE ELEMENTS FUN FACTS

## WHOPPER COPPER

**KNIVES AND FORKS, TEAPOTS AND PANS, EARRINGS AND BRACELETS** all can be formed out of rather soft and moldable copper. But copper can be used for more than just style; it's used as wire to conduct electricity through our homes and schools. The biggest piece of float copper (copper that has been carried away by glaciers from the place where it formed) in the world was found in 1997 in Michigan, U.S.A., by two men with a metal detector. It is estimated to weigh around 28 tons (25 t), which is about the weight of four or five elephants!

THE LARGEST PIECE OF FLOAT COPPER EVER FOUND WAS IN MICHIGAN.

## ANTIMONY THEN AND NOW

**ANTIMONY IS A BLUE-WHITE ELEMENT** that people used in ancient Egypt as an eyeliner. Today, it's used in batteries and as a flame retardant. Most natural antimony comes from China, but no new deposits have been found for more than 10 years. Since we can't make antimony in the lab, we may run out of natural antimony soon.

AN ANCIENT EGYPTIAN PAPYRUS PAINTING SHOWING HOW ANTIMONY WAS USED AS EYELINER

## COLD FIRE

**HENNIG BRAND DISCOVERED PHOSPHORUS IN GERMANY** in 1669 and nicknamed it "cold fire" because it glows in the dark. It was later also nicknamed "the devil's element" because phosphorus is explosive and is the 13th element that was discovered. It produces a greenish light when it mixes with oxygen in the air, so it's not surprising that phosphorus is used in flares.

PHOSPHORUS IS PAINTED ON THIS COMPASS TO MAKE IT GLOW IN THE DARK.

PHOSPHORUS GLOWS GREEN

## Semimetals

Semimetallic native elements have characteristics that fall between those of the metallic and nonmetallic elements. For instance, some semimetals have a shiny luster; others are dull. Semimetallic elements usually can conduct electricity, but not as well as metallic elements. Some semimetallic native elements include arsenic, antimony, and silicon.

## Nonmetals

Other than graphite, which is shiny and made of carbon, nonmetallic elements are nothing like metallic elements. Nonmetallic elements are lightweight and at least somewhat see-through. They are mostly brittle and can't be shaped. Some of the nonmetallic native elements are hydrogen, carbon, nitrogen, oxygen, phosphorus, sulfur, and selenium.

A SILICON WAFER CONDUCTS ELECTRICITY. SILICON IS USED IN MANY MODERN ELECTRONICS.

## Sulfides

The sulfides make up another mineral group. These minerals are made of sulfur combined with at least one metal or semimetal.

Sulfur is all around us. It's actually one of the most plentiful elements in the universe. It arrives on Earth via volcanic gas and is often found near volcano vents. Sulfur is bright yellow, and it doesn't have an odor ... except when it forms compounds such as the explosive poisonous gas called hydrogen sulfide. Then it has a stinky rotten-egg odor. The horrible-smelling spray from skunks and the stinky smell that comes from passing gas are all due to some form of sulfur. Sometimes you can smell sulfur in fertilizers and in the powder we use to shoot off fireworks.

But sulfur isn't used just for smelly or explosive purposes. It's in some of our medicines and foods, too. People soak in the healing waters of sulfur-filled hot springs.

BRASS IS A NATIVE ALLOY THAT WE CAN USE TO MAKE INSTRUMENTS.

THE SULFIDE PYRITE IS CALLED FOOL'S GOLD BECAUSE IT LOOKS VERY SIMILAR TO REAL GOLD.

Sulfur is added to rubber to make it stronger and more durable. This vulcanized rubber is used to make such things as hoses, tires, bowling balls, and hockey pucks. Sulfur itself is yellow, but many of the sulfide minerals are colorful. Let's take a look at some of the members of the sulfide group.

The sulfide mineral galena is made of lead and sulfur and is one of the main sources of lead. It has a metallic shine that can become gray and dull when exposed to air, it's soft, and the lead in it makes it dense and heavy. Galena is a mineral that has perfect cleavage in three directions, and its six- and eight-sided crystals give it a fun squared-off geometric shape. Galena doesn't always contain just lead. Argentiferous galena contains some silver impurities and is sometimes mined for its silver.

We've already discussed pyrite—fool's gold—which is Earth's most common sulfide. Although often mistaken for gold, pyrite looks and acts quite differently. For example, both gold and pyrite are shiny and yellowish, but gold is more of a golden yellow, whereas pyrite is a brassy, brighter yellow. Pyrite's streak is black with a greenish tint, but gold leaves golden flakes as its streak. Gold is a valuable precious mineral, whereas pyrite is hardly worth a penny. Sometimes, though, pyrite is formed into jewelry.

The name "pyrite" comes from the Greek word *pyr,* which means "fire." Sparks sputter when pyrite is struck by something hard, such as metal, and it can be used to start fires. Pyrite is also used to make sulfuric acid and is found in coal. When burned, sulfuric acid can contribute to acid rain.

Cinnabar is a mercury sulfide and can be found around active volcanoes and hot springs. Its bright red color is hard to miss. Like many brightly colored things in nature, cinnabar is toxic.

EVEN BOWLING BALLS CONTAIN A MINERAL: SULFUR!

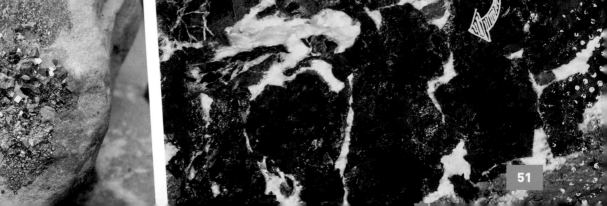

THE MERCURY SULFIDE CINNABAR IS BLOODRED.

IN THE BINGHAM CANYON MINE, PEOPLE MINE COPPER ORES—275,000 TONS (250,000 t) OF REFINED COPPER EVERY DAY, IN FACT! THAT WEIGHS MORE THAN 100,000 AFRICAN ELEPHANTS!

THE BINGHAM CANYON MINE, NEAR SALT LAKE CITY, UTAH, U.S.A.

# DIGGING FOR TREASURE

**ORES ARE MINERALS CONTAINING METALS** that can be removed from the ground and sold at a profit. Many of these minerals are sulfides and oxides. The sulfide galena, which contains lead, and the oxide hematite, which contains iron, are examples of ores. People get these valuable minerals by digging into the ground or using explosives to carve out mines. Mines can be deep tunnels underground or open pits or scraped land. In a simplified sense, a riverbed where you can pan for gold can be considered a mine.

Once the ore is hauled out of the ground, the valuable metal is removed from it through various heat, chemical, or electrical processes. And finally, the metal is manufactured into products, such as electronic equipment or jewelry, and sold.

GALENA CONTAINS LEAD, A TYPE OF ORE.

**MARS'S NICKNAME IS THE RED PLANET** because it sports a reddish hue. It turns out that the surface of Mars is littered with hematite, and it's the hematite and its iron content that turns Mars red. A gray hematite has also been spotted on Mars's surface. On Earth, gray hematite is often found in standing water or in hot springs. That's why some scientists think that finding gray hematite on Mars is proof that water once existed on the red planet. Water is needed for life to exist, so maybe long, long ago, Martians walked upon the surface of Mars.

THIS GRAY HEMATITE ON MARS MIGHT BE EVIDENCE THAT WATER ONCE EXISTED ON THE RED PLANET.

That's why even though its brilliant color inspired people to carve it into jewelry and use it in paints and dyes, it's no longer used in decorations.

Cinnabar grows on rock surfaces and is more often found in clusters than as crystals. The clusters are a dull red, quite different from the shiny bright red luster that its crystals show off.

Being a mercury sulfide, it's not surprising that cinnabar is mined for its mercury. To get the mercury out of cinnabar, it's heated in a furnace until the mercury-filled vapor drifts from the mineral and condenses into liquid mercury. If you recall, mercury is the only mineral that's a liquid at room temp-erature. (Well, ice is, too, but it's water at room temperature, and water is not a mineral.)

ANCIENT EGYPTIAN HIEROGLYPHS PAINTED WITH HEMATITE

## Oxides

The next mineral group is oxides. Oxides are compounds of oxygen and one or more metallic elements. A lot of oxides can form when an element reacts to oxygen. This is known as oxidation. There's so much oxygen on Earth, and it can combine with so many elements, that oxides come in a lot of different forms. They can be soft or hard. They can be drab or transparent. They can even be some of the most colorful, sparkly, and eye-catching minerals on Earth. Hematite, cuprite, and rutile are all oxides.

Hematite is an iron oxide. Economically, it's one of the most important ores of iron, but it's used for other things, too. It even has a history of being used as pigment. Hematite was used in ancient times as ink to paint hieroglyphs.

Just like oxides in general, hematite minerals have many different looks. They can be shiny or dull, and their colors range from red and brown to gray and silver. Hematite takes many shapes, including fibrous, or needlelike. But one thing stays the same no matter the mineral's shape or color: Its streak is always a shade of red. Hematite got its name from the Greek *haimatites lithos,* which means "bloodred stone."

# 2-FOR-1 MINERALS!

**MALACHITE AND AZURITE ARE CARBONATES** that are often found together, sometimes even with their green and blue crystals combined into what people call azurmalachite. They're both copper ores; malachite gets its green coloring from its copper. The striking banding within malachite is caused by small, dense, and fibrous needlelike crystals. It isn't worthwhile to mine malachite for its copper anymore, because there isn't enough copper in it. But it is polished into beautiful jewelry and other decorative pieces. Malachite hardly forms crystals and has a more rounded appearance than azurite, which does form crystals. Azurite is such a striking color that a shade of blue, called azure, was named after it.

AZURMALACHITE IS ACTUALLY TWO COPPER ORES: AZURITE AND MALACHITE.

A CLOSE-UP OF A GREEN COPPER ORE

Cuprite is a copper oxide and, not surprisingly, a source of copper. Sometimes called ruby copper, cuprite is red with a brick-red streak. At times, though, its red color is so dark that it looks black.

Different varieties of cuprite form crystals of different shapes. One type of cuprite called chalcotrichite forms needlelike fibrous crystals that make it look fuzzy.

Rutile is a titanium oxide and an ore of titanium. Lightweight and strong, titanium is used to make things from eyeglass frames to medical equipment.

Rutile can be many different shapes, and it ranges in color from dark red to yellow to silver, reflecting like a mirror. It often forms needlelike patterns inside a growing crystal. The most famous example is the star sapphire, which is a sapphire with a star shape in its center. The rutile trapped within the sapphire is responsible for the star shape.

LIGHTWEIGHT TITANIUM ORES MAKE GREAT GOLF CLUBS.

## Carbonates

All minerals in the carbonate group are made of one carbon atom intertwined with three oxygen atoms that team up with one or more metals. Most carbonates are transparent or light in color. Most of them are on the soft side. And many can dissolve in water and get bubbly when exposed to some acids.

Maybe even more surprising is that carbonate minerals are plentiful in ocean water and are used by some sea animals, such as sea snails, clams, and mussels, to create their shells.

Carbonate minerals fall into one of three subgroups: calcite, dolomite, and aragonite. Let's take a look at a few examples from each category.

SEA ANIMALS SUCH AS THIS GIANT CLAM USE CARBONATES FROM THE WATER TO HELP FORM THEIR SHELLS.

## Calcite

One of the more common minerals, calcite is used in many different ways by people. For example, we mix it into fertilizers to neutralize the acid in soil, its calcium is used in medicine, and its white pigment is used in paints.

To find out if a mineral you're holding is calcite, just pour some vinegar over it. If it's calcite, the acidic vinegar will dissolve the calcium carbonate in the mineral and release carbon dioxide in the form of fizzy bubbles.

Minerals in the calcite group include calcite, gaspeite, magnesite, otavite, rhodochrosite, siderite, smithsonite, and sphaerocobaltite.

GASPEITE IS AN EXAMPLE OF A CALCITE MINERAL.

## Dolomite

What happens if you take the magnesium out of dolomite? You end up with a mineral that's a lot like calcite. One big difference, though, is that dolomite doesn't contain calcium carbonate. That means it won't bubble the way calcite does if an acid like vinegar is poured on it. Dolomite crystals are somewhat unusual in that they can cluster and form in the shape of a saddle. Dolomite can be used to make brick, glass, and ceramics. Other minerals in the dolomite group are ankerite, benstonite, dolomite, huntite, kutnohorite, minrecordite, and norsethite.

## Aragonite

Both aragonite and calcite have the same chemical formula. The difference is in the structure of their crystals. With its needlelike pyramid-shaped crystals, aragonite takes on a more interesting form than calcite. But aragonite is not as stable, and over time its crystals break down and it becomes calcite.

The aragonite group includes aragonite, cerussite, strontianite, and witherite.

# Sulfates

Sulfur and oxygen combine with at least one other element to make a sulfate mineral. Sulfates are usually found near Earth's surface and are typically pale to translucent and have a glassy luster.

This is a large group, but most of the minerals are not very common. The best known members of the sulfate group are gypsum, barite, and anhydrite.

Gypsum is a calcium sulfate, which is a combination of calcium, sulfur bound to oxygen, and water. It's often part of what's left over after lakes and oceans evaporate.

Gypsum is usually colorless but can be white or even other colors if it contains impurities. It's used to make cement and plaster, including the plaster of paris used to make casts for broken bones.

The sulfate known as barite is the main ore of the metal barium. It comes in a variety of colors and crystal habits, or shapes, and is heavy and dense for a nonmetallic mineral. It has a specific gravity of 4.5.

Barite can grow in spaces between sand grains and in sedimentary rock, forming oddly shaped masses. Often these masses look like flowers, so they got the nickname "barite roses."

Anhydrite is a calcium sulfate, and it is often confused with gypsum. It's no wonder, since the only difference between the two is that gypsum has water molecules and anhydrite doesn't. The Greek word *anhydrous*, which means "without water," was the inspiration for the waterless anhydrite's name.

A BARITE ROSE, FORMED IN SEDIMENTARY ROCK

THE WHITE SAND DUNES OF CUATRO CIÉNEGAS IN COAHUILA, MEXICO, CONTAIN GYPSUM.

# Phosphates

The phosphate minerals tend to be brightly colored, heavy, relatively hard, and brittle. They are made with a base of phosphorus and oxygen. The most widespread use of phosphates is as fertilizer, which adds nutrients to soil that plants need to stay healthy.

With its shades of bluish green, turquoise is one of the most stunning phosphates. Another phosphate, pyromorphite, crystallizes quickly, and wavellite takes interesting crystal forms.

Turquoise is a popular choice for jewelry and decorative pieces and has been used this way throughout many cultures across the centuries. The copper, aluminum, and phosphate that came together to make turquoise were all parts of other minerals.

Because of this, turquoise is considered to be a secondary mineral.

Pyromorphite is a soft, dense lead phosphate mineral that is sometimes mined for its lead. It's typically a bright green, but it can be white, gray, brown, or yellow as well. Its crystals are usually shaped like barrels that form in masses. Pyromorphite gets its name from the Greek *pyr,* meaning "fire," and *morphe,* meaning "form" because of how quickly it crystallizes from its melted state.

Wavellite is an aluminum phosphate mineral, and it is hiding a surprise. Its needlelike crystals fan out to form pinwheels that can be seen when the mineral is fractured. It's usually a light to dark green color.

PINWHEEL CRYSTALS IN FRACTURED WAVELLITE

THE PHOSPHATE TURQUOISE IS OFTEN USED IN JEWELRY.

GREEN PYROMORPHITE HAS BARREL-LIKE CRYSTALS.

HALIDE FORMATIONS—
ALSO KNOWN AS SALT!

THE WATER IN THE DEAD SEA IS SO SALTY THAT WHEN THE WATER EVAPORATES, HALITE CRYSTALLIZES TO FORM LARGE SALT COLUMNS IN THE WATER.

SALT FORMATIONS IN THE DEAD SEA IN ISRAEL

## Halides

Minerals in the halide group are made of a metallic element combined with either bromine, chlorine, fluorine, or iodine. Most halides are soft with a low specific gravity, and many are transparent. You're very familiar with the halide mineral halite. It's an everyday seasoning in most homes. Fluorite and atacamite, two more examples of halides, will round out our glimpse into this mineral group.

Halite is made of sodium and chlorine, and you know it as salt. Many halides dissolve in water, and halite is no exception. When salty sea water evaporates, for instance, halite crystallizes into a solid mineral. But halite isn't just for the

COLORFUL FLUORITE CRYSTALS

dinner table. People spread it on icy roads and sidewalks to prevent slipping, and it's used to preserve food. It's also an important nutrient we need to stay healthy. For instance, it helps us digest our food, and it soothes a sore throat when we mix it with water and gargle with it.

Fluorite is made of calcium and fluorine. It may not have as many uses as halite has, but it can be a lot more colorful. Although its crystals are transparent, they're tinted with impurities in the form of bits of elements, making fluorite one of the most colorful minerals, coming in shades of violet, blue, and many other colors. Sometimes the eye-popping colors can be brilliant. As a matter of fact, you could say that they glow. They are fluorescent. The word "fluorescent" actually comes from fluorite because fluorite was one of the first fluorescent objects that caught our ancestors' eye. Some fluorites even glow when heated.

Visit Blue John Cavern in Derbyshire, England, and you'll find a stunning site—Blue John fluorite. Blue John Cavern is one of the only places on Earth where you can find this blue-purple-and-yellow-banded mineral. The cavern was discovered around 2,000 years ago by the Romans. It is such a special mineral that Blue John fluorite is mined by hand with crowbars and chisels—no blasting allowed.

Atacamite is a copper halide mineral that forms when copper is exposed to oxygen. It grows in arid, desertlike places and was named after the Atacama Desert in Chile, one of the driest places in the world. Atacamite comes in all shades of green and leaves an apple green streak. It is fairly rare, and it's used mostly in jewelry.

## Silicates

Minerals in the silicate group are made of silicon and oxygen and one or more additional elements, usually a metal. Making up about 95 percent of the upper mantle and crust, silicon and oxygen are the most widespread elements on Earth. It's no surprise, then, that the silicate group includes more minerals than any other mineral group. The quartzes are the stars of this group, mainly because they are the most recognizable.

Being such a large group, the silicates are divided into subgroups based on their structure, which is $SiO_4$. The four oxygen atoms surround the one silicon atom, forming the shape of a

# GLOW IN THE DARK

ADAMITE WILL GLOW IF YOU SHINE AN ULTRAVIOLET LIGHT ON IT.

**WHAT DO YOU GET WHEN** you go into a dark room with a fluorescent mineral and shine an ultraviolet light on it? A glowing mineral! We've already looked at the fluorescent mineral fluorite. Some other fluorescent minerals include adamite and gypsum. Even some geodes are fluorescent. Under ultraviolet light, also known as black light, fluorescent minerals glow in spectacularly bright colors. Fluorite, for instance, glows blue and violet. This glow comes from elements in fluorescent minerals called activators that glow in response to the ultraviolet light.

We can't see ultraviolet light because it's at a wavelength that is invisible to the human eye. But we can see its effects. Ultraviolet light gets absorbed by fluorescent minerals and then is released at a different wavelength, producing a different color, one that we can see. Some minerals have fluorescence strong enough that just holding them in the sunlight and then moving them into the shade is enough to make their activators glow.

CALCITE GLOWS RED, WILLEMITE GLOWS GREEN, AND FRANKLINITE IS BLACK UNDER ULTRAVIOLET LIGHT.

triangular pyramid called a tetrahedron. The arrangements of these tetrahedrons determine which subgroup the mineral is placed in. The tetrahedron can be arranged in six ways: single, double, chains, sheets, three-dimensional frameworks, or rings. These tetrahedron silicates are then organized into six subgroups:

1. Cyclosilicates
2. Inosilicates
3. Nesosilicates
4. Phyllosilicates
5. Sorosilicates
6. Tectosilicates

The cyclosilicate tetrahedrons form a ring. Beryl is an example of a cyclosilicate. It's a hexagon-shaped glassy crystal that comes in a variety of colors. And depending on its color, beryl goes by other names, such as emerald and aquamarine.

The inosilicate tetrahedrons form single or double chains. Jadeite is an example of an inosilicate. You may know this mineral by the name jade. But what we loosely call jade can be an aggregate, or combination, of a few minerals. Only jadeite is a true jade.

Jade has been important in Chinese culture since ancient times. It has been crafted into jewelry and decorative pieces all over the world for thousands of years. It's not green, though, it's white. Again, it's the impurities that give jadeite its color, which can be lilac, yellow, or green.

Nesosilicates are formed by a single tetrahedron, so they are sometimes called island silicates. And being a single tetrahedron, nesosilicates have the simplest structure of all the silicates. Topaz is a type of nesosilicate. It has large prism-shaped crystals. Topaz is usually golden yellow but can be brown, red, pink, or gray. People create jewelry and other decorative pieces with topaz.

The phyllosilicates are formed by tetrahedrons that are arranged in sheets. The minerals in this group are often soft and flaky. The softest mineral with a hardness rating of 1 is a phyllosilicate—talc. Talc has many uses, including as laboratory table tops and as fillers in some plastics and paints.

The sorosilicates are silicate minerals formed by two tetrahedrons. It's the smallest silicate subgroup, and most of its minerals are rare. Hemimorphite is made of crystals that are different at each end. One end is flat, and the other is either rounded or pointed. The rounded end can look globular and lumpy, like a group of grapes.

Making up about 75 percent of Earth's crust are the tectosilicates, which are made of a strong framework of molecules. Quartz, itself one of the most plentiful of all the minerals, is a tectosilicate.

THE NESOSILICATE TOPAZ IS OFTEN USED IN JEWELRY.

HERE, GREEN JADE IS CARVED INTO ORNAMENTS.

It comes in a rainbow of colors depending on the other bits of elements, or impurities, it has. The purple color in quartz known as amethyst comes from a bit of iron and manganese mixed into the mineral. Amethyst is often found inside geodes. Most sand is made of quartz, and a type of quartz called flint was carved into arrowheads by Native Americans.

## Gemstones

Gemstones sparkle with color and light and are used to decorate art, furniture, military weapons (as a sign of high rank), and even ourselves. They are minerals that dazzle us with their beauty. But if you go out hunting for gemstones, don't search for eye-catching color and shine. That's because in their natural state, gemstones look like ordinary rocks. It isn't until they're cut and polished that gemstones get their bling.

So what is a gemstone? Simply, a gemstone is rare and made of one or more minerals. People value gemstones for their beauty and have divided them into two categories: precious and semi-precious. Precious gemstones are highly valued and are worth a lot of money. Semiprecious gemstones are not as highly valued, and they're not worth as much money as precious gems are. The list of precious gemstones is short—diamonds, emeralds, rubies, and sapphires.

ROUGH EMERALDS CAN BE CUT INTO GEMSTONES.

Some gemologists, scientists who study gems, put pearls and opals on the precious gems list. But pearls are organic, made by living oysters, so by definition they're not minerals. And opals don't have crystals, so they aren't true minerals, either. They're called mineraloids. Scientists disagree about whether other organic gems should be classified as mineraloids. Organic gems include amber, which is fossilized tree sap; coral; sand dollars; jet; and even dinosaur bones. Because of these gray areas of classification, organic gems are now categorized much like other minerals are, by their physical properties. Special laboratories around the world make it their business to classify organic gems and grade their quality.

## JET-BLACK

**JET IS AN ORGANIC GEM.** It is somewhat like coal because it starts out as a woody material. Then it gets buried in debris on the ground called sediment, and over thousands of years, it hardens into a gem that can be cut and polished to a shiny jet-black color. As a matter of fact, the "jet" in the phrase "jet-black" refers to this gem.

POLISHED JET IS SMOOTH AND HAS SHINE.

RAW JET LOOKS ALMOST LIKE THE WOODY MATERIAL IT USED TO BE.

# MODERN BIRTHSTONES

**ONE OF THE MOST FAMILIAR GROUPINGS OF GEMS ARE BIRTHSTONES.** Their origins go back for centuries, and their significance has changed throughout history. At one point, it was believed that each gem had particular healing properties. When people wore the corresponding gem during their birthday month, those healing properties were strengthened. Since that time, a slightly different list of birthstones has come out. Some months have more than one birthstone because some gemstones are either too rare or not very popular. Here are the birthstones we use today:

**JANUARY: GARNET**

REPRESENTS TRUST, FRIENDSHIP; BELIEVED TO PROTECT PEOPLE DURING TRAVELS

**APRIL: DIAMOND**

REPRESENTS LOVE, MARRIAGE, COURAGE

**MAY: EMERALD**

REPRESENTS REBIRTH, FERTILITY, HEALTH, FAITHFULNESS, FORESIGHT, YOUTH, GOOD FORTUNE

**AUGUST: PERIDOT**

REPRESENTS STRENGTH; BELIEVED TO PROTECT AGAINST NIGHTMARES, EVILS, ENCHANTMENTS

**SEPTEMBER: SAPPHIRE**

REPRESENTS WISDOM, PURITY, FAITH; BELIEVED TO PROTECT LOVED ONES FROM HARM

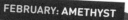

**FEBRUARY: AMETHYST**

REPRESENTS SERENITY, ROYALTY, COURAGE; BELIEVED TO STRENGTHEN RELATIONSHIPS

**MARCH: AQUAMARINE**

PROMOTES YOUTH, HEALTH, HOPE, LOVE; BELIEVED TO HEAL HEART, LIVER, AND STOMACH

**JULY: RUBY**

REPRESENTS LOVE, PASSION, WEALTH, PEACE; BELIEVED TO PROTECT AGAINST EVIL AND HARM

**JUNE: ALEXANDRITE**

BELIEVED TO PROMOTE HEIGHTENED INTUITION, PLEASURE

**NOVEMBER: TOPAZ, CITRINE**

A SIGN OF LOVE AND AFFECTION; BELIEVED TO PROTECT HEALTH AND HELP EYESIGHT

**OCTOBER: TOURMALINE**

BELIEVED TO REPRESENT LUCK IN SOME CULTURES AND MISFORTUNE IN OTHERS

**DECEMBER: TANZANITE**

BELIEVED TO RELIEVE PAIN AND BOOST APPETITE

# ROCK OUT!

## CRYSTAL CANDY

You can grow crystals and have a treat at the same time! For this experiment, you will need an adult's help because you'll be boiling water. But when you're done, you'll be able to eat your experiment.

ASK AN ADULT TO HELP YOU HANDLE THE BOILING HOT WATER.

## What you need:

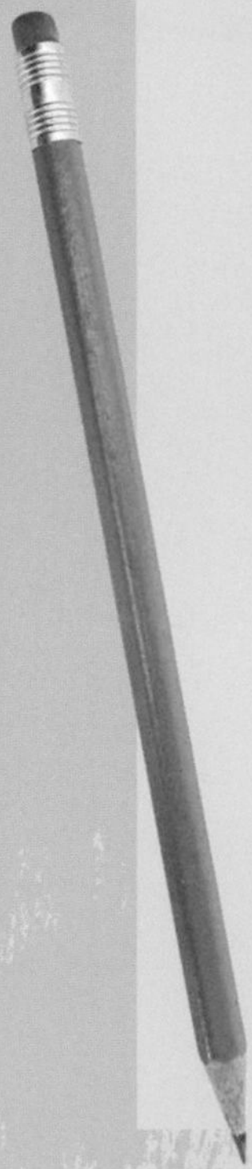

1 clean glass jar or drinking glass

1 non-nylon string or yarn shorter than your jar or glass

1 pencil

1 cup (235 mL) water

1 saucepan

1 spoon for stirring

3 cups (594 g) table sugar

Food coloring (optional)

TABLE SUGAR

## What to do:

1. **Tie the string to the middle of the pencil.** Test to make sure the string hangs into your jar without touching the bottom or sides when the pencil is set across the top of the jar. Remove the pencil and string from the jar.

2. **Ask an adult to help you** pour the water into the saucepan, place it on the stove, turn the heat on high, and bring the water to a boil.

3. **Lower the heat to a simmer, and slowly stir in the sugar so it dissolves before you add more.** If you see that the sugar isn't dissolving, that means the solution is saturated, and the water can't absorb any more sugar. Make sure you have adult supervision.

4. **Have an adult help you add a few drops of food coloring** if you want your crystal candy to be colorful, and stir it into the sugar water.

5. **Ask an adult to pour the solution from the saucepan into the jar.** Stand back and be careful because the water will be boiling hot.

6. **Balance the pencil across the top of the jar,** and make sure the string is dangling into the solution. Do not let the string hit the sides or bottom of the jar.

7. **Find a safe, out-of-the-way place** to put your jar so it won't get bumped or exposed to a lot of dust.

**Note: If your jar isn't perfectly clean or if there are undissolved sugar crystals in your solution, the candy crystals will grow on the dirt and the undissolved sugar crystals, not on the string.**

8. **Let your crystal candy grow undisturbed for a few days.** Check on it once in a while so you can see how the crystals are forming. When your crystal candy stops growing or when it's as big as you want it to be, take it out of the jar, put it aside on a plate, and let it dry. Once it's dry, you can eat your treat!

TALL COLUMNS OF BASALT ROCK IN SANTA MARÍA REGLA PARK, IN HUASCA DE OCAMPO, MEXICO. THE PRISM SHAPES WERE FORMED AS LAVA SLOWLY COOLED.

CHAPTER 3

ROCKS UNDER PRESSURE

# INTRODUCTION

## I GET TO DO MY RESEARCH IN UNUSUAL PARTS OF THE WORLD.

It's one of the bonuses of being a geophysicist. I usually travel with a team of scientists. We set up instruments that will give us information about whatever it is we're researching at the time.

DR. SARAH STAMPS

On this trip, we were in Serengeti National Park, in Tanzania, Africa. We had spent the day searching the grasslands of the Serengeti for a strong rock that we could use to take measurements with our instruments. We wanted to measure the movement of Earth's crust and how tectonic plates shift. We were looking for a rock at the surface that extends very deep within Earth, because we needed the rock to represent crust movement, not just movement of the soil or sediment that it was in. We finally found a hard metamorphic rock called gneiss (pronounced like nice) sticking out of the ground. We set up our instruments, which included a GPS antenna, GPS receiver, solar panel, battery, and all the parts that connect everything. Now we needed to find a place to stay while we collected the data. We went to take a look at a house where only researchers stay. My team went in and started checking things out, and I was the last

person into the house. But I was being followed—by a baboon! And he was a big one. He must have been about four feet (1 m) tall. He was not the kind of baboon you'd want to mess with.

He walked in, stood there, and stared at me. My first thought was to get him out, and I stepped toward him to see if I could scare him. It might not have been the best idea, but I did it anyway. He flinched, but then just stared me down. I thought, *Okay, now what am I going to do?* I looked around and saw a broom, grabbed it, and ran at him. That finally scared him out.

When we eventually went back out to our car, we couldn't believe what we saw. All the food in our car had been stolen by the big baboon's band of monkeys. The leader had come into the house to distract us while the other baboons stole all our food!

It's a good thing we weren't scared away by the baboons. The information we gathered from measuring the gneiss is very interesting. In many places in Tanzania, we measured Earth movements that are east-west in orientation. These movements make sense given our understanding of African plate tectonics. However, the Serengeti GPS site shows a very strange northward movement that we are still trying to figure out.

YELLOW BABOONS LIKE THIS ONE ARE FOUND THROUGHOUT TANZANIA.

FOR HER RESEARCH, DR. STAMPS LOOKS FOR BEDROCK—ROCK THAT EXTENDS VERY DEEP DOWN INTO THE EARTH.

SERENGETI NATIONAL PARK, IN TANZANIA, WHERE DR. STAMPS AND HER CREW CONDUCTED RESEARCH

# WHEN YOU THINK OF A ROCK, YOU PROBABLY PICTURE AN ORDINARY, DULL GRAY OR BROWN STONE.

But look closely at two rocks, and you'll probably see differences in texture (are they smooth or rough?), color, and maybe even hardness.

These traits are clues to a rock's history. And because rocks are part of Earth, these traits are clues to Earth's history, too.

We already know there are three types of rocks. Igneous rock comes from the cooling of magma and lava. Sedimentary rock is made up of bits and pieces of other rocks on Earth's crust. And metamorphic rock forms deep underground, where high temperatures and pressure change existing rocks into new and different rocks. Although 95 percent of Earth's crust is made of igneous and metamorphic rock, 75 percent of the rocks we find on Earth's surface are sedimentary rocks.

## Igneous Rocks

Rocks on Earth, every single one of them, began as igneous rocks. They form from the cooling and hardening of fiery-hot magma, which originates in Earth's mantle. Saying the magma is fiery hot is not an exaggeration. It reaches temperatures of 1100 to 2400°F (600 to 1315°C), which is pretty much the temperature of fire—some fires, such as candle flames, can get hotter. Magma isn't just melted rocks. In fact, magma's ingredients include solid rocks, crystallized minerals, and gases that have dissolved into a hot, gooey mass.

Igneous rocks are divided into two major categories, and rocks in each category form in different parts of Earth. Intrusive igneous rocks (also called plutonic) form underground. They cool slowly, taking thousands, even millions of years for their temperatures to drop. This allows time for the crystals to grow before the rocks harden. Bigger crystals make a grainier, more roughly textured rock, like granite. Extrusive (also called volcanic) rocks are ejected or flow onto Earth's surface, cooling quickly in a matter of days or months. This quick cooling doesn't give crystals much time to grow, so crystals remain small in extrusive rocks. The small crystals give extrusive rocks a finer grain with a smooth texture, like that of basalt. Now that we have a general idea of what intrusive and extrusive rocks are, let's take a look at some of the different types of rocks that make up each category.

A BUST OF PLUTO, ROMAN GOD OF THE UNDERWORLD, AFTER WHOM "PLUTONIC" ROCKS WERE NAMED

## Intrusive (Plutonic) Igneous Rocks

Named after Pluto, the Roman god of the underworld, plutonic rocks form slowly underground as magma cools. They tend to have a rough texture and large crystals that you can actually see without the help of a microscope. Because the rocks form underground, it isn't until they're blasted out of a volcano or exposed through weathering or erosion that they see the light of day.

THE INTERESTING ROCKY SHAPES AT THE GIANT'S CAUSEWAY WERE FORMED 60 MILLION YEARS AGO AS MAGMA SEEPED THROUGH FISSURES IN EARTH'S CRUST.

THE BASALT COLUMNS AT THE GIANT'S CAUSEWAY IN NORTHERN IRELAND LOOK HEXAGONAL IN SHAPE.

# THE GIANT'S CAUSEWAY

**ACCORDING TO IRISH LEGEND,** people worked with picks and shovels to carve out the 40,000 mostly hexagonal steps or columns on the coast of County Antrim in Northern Ireland. Or was it the giant named Finn McCool who built these steps into the sea to fight a Scottish giant named Benandonner? Both of these stories had made perfect sense. How else could these almost perfect, tightly packed columns have been formed? Then science proved that it was all nature's doing.

Around 60 million years ago, magma was forced between the boundaries of moving tectonic plates in the area of Northern Ireland. Once the magma reached Earth's surface, the lava cooled quickly. Then water seeped through, creating cracks and forming these amazing columns of igneous rock called columnar basalt. The columns can be massively tall, reaching heights of 36 feet (11 m). That's about as tall as a four-story building.

ACCORDING TO CELTIC LEGEND, THE GIANT FINN McCOOL WAS A WARRIOR.

BIOTITE, A MICA MINERAL THAT IS ALSO RESPONSIBLE FOR ADDING BLACK TO GRANITE, HAS TABULAR CRYSTALS ARRANGED LIKE A PAD OF PAPER.

MOST OF THE MINERALS IN EARTH'S CRUST ARE SOME SORT OF FELDSPAR, LIKE THIS ORTHOCLASE, WHICH CAN BE WHITE, YELLOW, OR PINK.

OLIVINE MINERALS LIKE THESE ARE COMMON IN THE UPPER MANTLE OF EARTH'S CRUST AND ARE ALSO FOUND AS LARGE GRAINS IN METEORITES. THEY GOT THEIR START IN OUTER SPACE!

Granite is the intrusive igneous rock that people are most likely to recognize. It is also the most common rock, making up almost three-quarters of Earth's crust. Granite is made mostly of feldspars and quartzes, and it may have a number of other minerals mixed in. Granite is a light-colored rock, often with salt-and-pepper speckles of black and sometimes other colors. The colors, including black, come from other minerals in the granite. A type of mica called biotite is one of the main minerals that adds black to granite. A granite that is mostly pink likely got its color from a pink feldspar called orthoclase.

Diorite is another large-crystal intrusive rock that can be described as having salt-and-pepper coloring. Even though it may look a lot like granite, diorite is made up of different minerals. The biggest difference is that diorite has very little, if any, quartz. Instead, it's made up mostly of feldspars that contain calcium and sodium called plagioclase feldspars. And diorite may contain the mineral hornblende instead of biotite. The dark green color that diorite sometimes sports is caused by hornblende.

People have managed to carve sculptures out of diorite despite its hardness. And diorite can be cut and polished to be used as jewelry. The ancient Inca of South America and ancient Maya of Mexico and Central America built structures with diorite. And we continue to use diorite to this day in construction.

Gabbro is a black to dark green rock mostly made up of plagioclase feldspar, which has a lot of calcium and the mineral augite. It's on the heavy side, since it does contain some iron. But it doesn't have much quartz, which is unusual for an igneous rock.

Basalt is gabbro's twin because they are identical in composition. The difference between the two is that gabbro is an intrusive igneous rock and basalt is extrusive, exploding or flowing onto

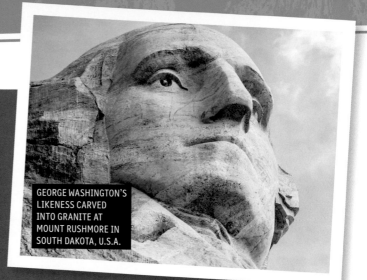

# MOUNT RUSHMORE

**GRANITE IS SUCH A STRONG ROCK** that it's been used for all types of industrial purposes, including as a building material. But it has also been carved into historical monuments.

Mount Rushmore, a 5,600-foot (1,707-m) mountain in the Black Hills of South Dakota, U.S.A., is famous for the faces of four United States presidents that were carved into its side. In the 1920s, dynamite blasted away part of the hard granite mountain, a necessary step in the preparation for the carvings. Little by little, the 60-foot (18-meter)-tall faces of presidents George Washington, Thomas Jefferson, Theodore Roosevelt, and Abraham Lincoln were carved. The mountain's granite is so hard that it will take 10,000 years for one inch (2.5 cm) of the presidential faces to weather away.

GEORGE WASHINGTON'S LIKENESS CARVED INTO GRANITE AT MOUNT RUSHMORE IN SOUTH DAKOTA, U.S.A.

Earth and cooling quickly. Because basalt cools more rapidly than gabbro, basalt's grains are finer. And while basalt is the main rock of ocean floors, gabbro is the main rock deeper in Earth's crust.

Pegmatite is a group of intrusive igneous rocks that is similar to granite but has extremely big crystals. The smallest crystals are about a half inch (1 cm) in diameter. But the biggest pegmatites have been found with crystals that are more than 40 feet (12 m) long and 5 feet (1.5 m) in diameter!

So now you're thinking that extreme pegmatite crystals must have grown really slowly, since crystals need time to grow big. But there is a different reason these crystals grew so large. Dissolved water and other substances, such as chlorine, boron, and beryllium, that easily vaporize (turn to gas) get mixed in with magma when it's just beginning to crystallize. The substances allow only a few crystals to grow, so the crystals can grow big. This is how it works.

Toward the end of the crystallization process, water builds up and forms water pockets that get separated from the hardening magma. Atoms of the other substances bounce around these pockets of superhot water, which allows them to form giant-size crystals quickly. Some of these bouncing atoms are those of rare minerals and gems such as aquamarine, corundum (ruby and sapphire), and tourmaline.

Like pegmatite, peridotite is not just one rock; it describes a group of rocks. Peridotite rocks are dark in color and have coarse grains. They usually contain the mineral olivine, which tints many of these rocks green.

Peridotite is an intrusive igneous rock that is usually forced upward onto Earth's surface through natural means called kimberlite pipes and ophiolites. Ophiolites are parts of Earth's oceanic crust that have been moved up onto the overlying continental crust and convergent plate boundaries. They bring peridotite up to Earth's surface. By analyzing the material that surfaces with peridotite, scientists have determined it is one of the main rocks in the mantle.

# FELSIC VS. MAFIC

**GEOLOGISTS HAVE A VARIETY OF WAYS TO ORGANIZE ROCKS.**
One general way is to divide them into felsic and mafic, which describe their silica content and general color and mineral composition. Felsic rocks are found on the continental crust. They are made of feldspar minerals and quartzes, which have a lot of silica. Silica is made of silicon and oxygen. Most felsic rocks are light in color and in weight. Examples of felsic rocks are granite and pumice. Mafic rocks are found on ocean floors. They are mostly made of magnesium and iron. Most mafic rocks are heavy and dark in color. Basalt and gabbro are examples of mafic rocks.

A CLOSE-UP OF GRANITE, A TYPE OF FELSIC ROCK

A CLOSE-UP OF BASALT, A TYPE OF MAFIC ROCK

The other natural way peridotite reaches Earth's surface is through kimberlite pipes. Kimberlite is a type of peridotite, and a pipe is a funnel-shaped chimney that reaches from the mantle to the crust. In the upper mantle, peridotite is heated and squeezed under pressure until it partially melts and becomes magma. Gases and water push the magma upward through kimberlite pipes. Minerals start to crystallize, gases expand, and pressure increases. More and more pressure builds, and xenoliths get torn from the mantle and carried along with the magma. Xenoliths are fragments of rocks that were trapped in magma as it cooled. Peridotite is typically found in xenoliths. Pressure continues to build until the kimberlite is traveling a speedy 1,200 feet (370 m) per second. More rock is torn away from the pipe's sides and is swept up with the magma until it explodes in an eruption,

DIAMOND IN THE ROUGH

A DIAMOND EMBEDDED IN KIMBERLITE

ejecting lava violently or as a gentle flow. Don't hold your breath waiting to see this type of eruption. The last one took place more than 25 million years ago.

There's one very bright side effect of these eruptions from deep within Earth's mantle: diamonds. Magma transported through kimberlite pipes forms up to 100 miles (160 km) below Earth's surface. The pressure and temperatures are high enough deep within Earth for carbon to crystallize into diamonds. At shallower depths under less pressure and at lower temperatures, carbon can form into graphite. Some of the xenoliths being torn from the surrounding mantle during a kimberlite pipe eruption contain diamonds and are diamonds' best way to get to Earth's surface. Kimberlite is named after Kimberley, South Africa, the area where most of the world's kimberlite pipes are located.

A MARINE IGUANA PERCHES ON EXTRUSIVE IGNEOUS ROCK ON SANTIAGO ISLAND IN THE GALÁPAGOS.

## Extrusive (Volcanic) Igneous Rocks

Although xenoliths containing peridotite erupt onto Earth's surface through natural kimberlite pipes, the xenoliths had formed and crystallized within Earth's mantle. So they keep their intrusive rock status. Igneous rocks that cool and crystallize after magma reaches Earth's surface as lava are called extrusive igneous rocks. These rocks have small crystals, fine grains, or even no crystals at all. Those rocks that have no crystals at all are said to be glassy because of their smooth and shiny texture. As some extrusive rocks cool, hot gases can be trapped within, forming visible bubbles.

COOLED VOLCANIC LAVA SHOWS BUBBLES AS WELL AS DIFFERENT METALS.

Basalt is a dark-colored extrusive rock. It forms a thin layer across ocean floors. But it can be found on land as well. The main minerals that make up basalt are magnesium and iron. Being an extrusive rock, basalt has fine grains that can't be seen by the naked eye. Basalt flows out of hot spots and shield volcanoes, such as those found on the islands of Hawaii and the Galápagos Islands. When a volcano erupts underwater, the lava cools quickly, forming rocks of basalt into pillow shapes that cool into volcanic glass.

Another rock that forms when magma erupts into water is a silica-rich volcanic glass called obsidian. Sometimes air bubbles get trapped as obsidian hardens, which decorates the black, purple, and dark green volcanic glass with colorful splotches and stripes. This volcanic glass gets worn away easily, so it's hard to find obsidian that's more than a few million years old.

Obsidian has been used by people in many ways throughout history. As long ago as 7000 B.C., ancient peoples primped in front of mirrors made of obsidian. Later, people realized that the broken edges of obsidian are sharp. This led to its widespread use as tools, such as knives and spears, during the Stone Age.

Even today, obsidian is used in sharp and precise surgical equipment. But obsidian's beauty hasn't been lost on us. Even though it's on the soft side, obsidian is cut, shaped, and polished into jewelry such as earrings and pins.

Andesite is a group of fine-grained gray extrusive rocks that typically erupt from composite volcanoes. Andesite is named after the Andes Mountains in South America, which is one of the places it can be found. It forms mostly above subduction zones, where a piece of dense ocean lithosphere moves underneath less dense continental lithosphere. Andesite is made up of plagioclase feldspar, sometimes biotite, and other minerals. Once in a while, some minerals in andesite begin to cool and crystallize while still underground. Then when it erupts, the rest of the minerals crystallize quickly. These andesite rocks are called andesite porphyry, and they end up having both big and small crystals.

What happens when air, water, and bubbles of different gases get mixed in with lava? As the gas escapes, the lava gets frothy. The minerals crystallize around the gases, forming a porous, almost lacy-looking, light and airy rock that floats. One such rock is pumice.

Although it can float in water, pumice is able to absorb, or soak up, liquid. While floating, it will absorb water and sink. Because of its absorbent ability, it is used in some kitty litters to soak up wastes. It's abrasive, too, so people can use it to scrub away callouses on feet and elbows. Pumice is also used in concrete, as decorative landscaping rock, and in heavy-duty soap.

Rhyolite is a gray or pink rock containing a lot of silica, with quartz, plagioclase feldspar, and bits of other minerals mixed in. It's made of the same minerals found in granite. But because granite is an intrusive rock and rhyolite is an extrusive rock, they look different. For instance, granite has large crystals, whereas rhyolite cools more quickly than granite and has crystals so small that you can't see them without magnification.

Sometimes gases get trapped in rhyolite lava and leave little holes as it rapidly cools. This type of rhyolite forms pumice. Sometimes crystals

PUMICE FORMS AS FROTHY LAVA COOLS, LEAVING A BUBBLY PATTERN.

# VOLCANIC GLASS
**EXTRUSIVE ROCKS THAT COOL REALLY QUICKLY LOOK GLASSY.** This is especially true if, after an eruption, the lava falls into water. These rocks look glassy because they've cooled too quickly for crystals to form. Since they don't have crystals, they're not classified as a mineral. Obsidian is an example of volcanic glass.

OBSIDIAN, ALSO KNOWN AS VOLCANIC GLASS

THE KARYMSKY VOLCANO IN RUSSIA ERUPTS IN A CLOUD OF ASH.

VOLCANIC ASH COVERS A ROW OF CARS AFTER AN ERUPTION.

## VOLCANIC ASH

**YOU'D THINK WITH A VOLCANIC ERUPTION,** the most you'd need to worry about is getting away from the lava flow. That certainly is important, but the ash that erupts from a volcano could pose an even more sinister danger.

Volcanic ash is not like the wood-burning ash you get in your fireplace or campfire. Unlike the light and fluffy ash you're used to, volcanic ash is made of tiny mineral and rock fragments. These fragments range from powdery to around the size of sand grains, and they're hard and rough. They're so hard, in fact, that volcanic ash rates more than a 5 on the Mohs scale of hardness.

These flows of ash and gas barrel down the sides of volcanoes at breakneck speeds, destroying everything in their path. Volcanic ash can be picked up by the wind and carried high into the air and for thousands of miles (km), causing damage along the way.

VOLCANIC ASH IS MADE UP OF SMALL BITS OF MINERALS AND ROCKS.

In areas near an eruption, the ash can be thick enough to block out the sun, turning day to night. It can bury cities and farmland under a few feet of ash. As it travels with the wind, volcanic ash can damage airplanes and crops, pollute the water supply, and even damage lungs and cause breathing problems. Ash can have an electrical charge that jumbles radio waves and interferes with TV, GPS, and cell phone signals. Ash particles rubbing together can also create lightning! Volcanic ash doesn't dissolve in water, so if it rains after an eruption, the ash builds up as a thick, muddy mess.

ARCHES NATIONAL PARK IN UTAH, U.S.A., IS HOME TO MORE THAN 2,000 SANDSTONE ARCHES. SANDSTONE IS A TYPE OF SEDIMENTARY ROCK.

SEDIMENTARY ROCKS LIKE THESE RIVER ROCKS ARE WORN DOWN BY EROSION FROM MOVING WATER.

and opals, even gemstones, can get lodged in these holes, making these rhyolites special to both rock and gem hunters alike.

When a volcano erupts, more than just magma bursts into the air. Rock fragments, hot ash, and other materials also go along for the ride. And sometimes when magma (now called lava because it has reached Earth's surface), rock, and ash hit Earth's surface, it avalanches down the side of the volcano. By the time everything cools and comes to a halt, the ash and other materials have been welded, or cemented, together, forming rocks such as tuff, an indigenous rock. Each eruption lays down a layer of rock that can eventually build up around the volcano. Yellowstone National Park is one place where you can see welded tuff.

## Sedimentary Rocks

Igneous rocks can be hot and churning and explosive and dynamic. Sedimentary rocks, on the other hand, do not rely on extreme heat or pressure; they form quietly on or near Earth's surface.

Sediment is made of natural materials that are left behind by wind, water, glaciers, and gravity. These forces of nature wear away, or weather, all kinds of rocks, dissolving them or breaking them down into tiny bits. Then gravity, running streams, wind, and moving glaciers finish the job with erosion, moving the weathered bits to be deposited on the floor of a body of water, such as a stream, river, lake, or ocean. The heaviest bits are the first to be deposited. Layer upon layer of sediment build up and, eventually, change to solid rock. But it doesn't happen overnight. Typically, thousands

CALCITE DEPOSITS ON A FAUCET

of years are needed to complete this process.

A sedimentary rock, then, is a layered rock that's formed by the compacting, cementing, or crystallizing of sediments. Let's take a closer look at what all this means.

As layers of sediment build, the top layers weigh down on the bottom layers. Pores in the sediment get squeezed, and water in the pores gets wrung out. The sediment grains get pressed tightly together and form solid rock. This is called compaction.

In cementation, the pores in the sediment are filled in with dissolved minerals. This mineral solution cements, or glues, the sediment grains together to form rock. Conglomerate is one example of a rock that forms through cementation.

You probably hardly ever come across a sharp, jagged-edged rock when you cross a stream or swim in an ocean or a lake. That's because the action of water flowing over, smashing onto, or even lapping up against rock rounds and smooths its surface. At the same time, this action wears away and dissolves some of the rock's minerals. When the water is saturated with minerals and no more minerals can dissolve, they crystallize, and over time the crystals build up and bind into sedimentary rock. You can see crystallization in action when hard white calcite from tap water builds up on your faucets at home.

Now that we understand what sedimentary rocks are and the various ways they form, let's look at different kinds of sedimentary rocks. Geologists organize sedimentary rocks into three groups: clastic, chemical, and organic.

# FOSSILS: REMAINS TO BE SEEN

BANDED SANDSTONE LAYERS IN THE GRAND CANYON IN ARIZONA

**FOSSILS PROVIDE A WINDOW INTO A BYGONE TIME** of dinosaurs and giant mammals. Some fossils are the only proof we have that an extinct species was ever alive. Fossils are the remains of ancient plants and animals that are preserved in rock, usually sedimentary rock. The remains can be parts of a dead organism's body, eggs, dung, nests, and footprints.

The best way for a fossil to form is for the plant or animal to be buried in sand or mud right after its death. The soft parts of the remains begin to rot and decompose, exposing the bones and teeth. Layers of sediment pile on top of these hard remains. The layers start to get heavy, and during thousands of years the pressure squeezes and hardens them into sedimentary rock. As even more time passes, minerals replace the bones and teeth, forming a model made of rock of the ancient creature. Sometimes, though, a fossil is an imprint, such as a footprint, that has been preserved in stone.

Fossils are buried within layers of sedimentary rock, so how do they get to Earth's surface where we find them? The answer is that fossils are brought to the surface through Earth's tectonic movements and exposed by the erosion of Earth's crust.

A FOSSIL OF THE BIRD-LIKE DINOSAUR ARCHAEOPTERYX

## Clastic Sedimentary Rocks

Clastic sedimentary rocks are made of pieces of minerals and rocks of any type that have been weathered or broken off of existing rock. When these bits and pieces are compacted or cemented, they become rock. Clastic rocks include sandstone, shale, conglomerate, and breccia.

Sandstone is a combination of minerals, bits of rock, and organic matter, such as leaves, twigs, and dead insects, that have been weathered and beaten into small grains. Wind, water, and ice carry these grains to low-lying areas. And that's where the grains are compacted or cemented into rock.

Sandstone is mostly feldspar and quartz ground into sand-size grains that are formed into solid rock. It's cemented mostly by calcite, silica, and gypsum. And it gets its colors from impurities, or trace elements, such as iron oxides and manganese oxides. Because

THIN LAYERS OF SHALE CAN BE RED, GRAY, BROWN, AND BLACK.

IN 2012, NASA'S ROVER CURIOSITY SNAPPED PICTURES OF CONGLOMERATE ROCKS ON MARS. PROOF OF CONGLOMERATE ROCKS ON MARS IS THE BEST EVIDENCE WE HAVE THAT WATER ONCE FLOWED ON THE PLANET'S SURFACE.

sandstone is layered, it can be banded with a range of colors, depending on the available rocks and minerals at the time it was formed. Many national parks, including the Grand Canyon, in Arizona, U.S.A., showcase spectacular sandstone features.

Shale is a clastic sedimentary rock made mainly of clay and silt that is slowly carried to ocean and river floors. It also contains minerals such as feldspar, quartz, pyrite, and mica, as well as organic matter of shells and dead sea plants and animals. Shale forms in thin layers that can split into sheets, and it comes in a variety of colors, including red, green, brown, gray, and black. Black organic shale can be a source of oil and natural gas. Shale's crystals are so tiny that you can't see them with your naked eye.

Conglomerate is a type of clastic

BRECCIA IS MADE OF MANY JAGGED PIECES OF OTHER TYPES OF ROCKS.

sedimentary rock made of a collection of fairly large rounded rocks that are cemented together. Strong waves or swift streams or rivers are required to tumble rocks into smoothness. Smaller grains of quartz, calcite, and other minerals fill in the spaces between the rounded rocks and act like a glue that cements the rocks together to form conglomerate.

Breccia is a rock that's a lot like conglomerate, but breccia's particles have sharp corners and are more jagged. This tells us that breccia hasn't gone through as much tumbling in water as conglomerate rock has. Like conglomerate, breccia can be made of a variety of rocks, so it comes in many different colors. The more colorful and striking examples of breccia are often polished and cut into gemstones to be worn as jewelry.

## Chemical Sedimentary Rocks

Instead of forming from pressed bits of sediment, chemical sedimentary rocks start out as sediments dissolved in water. They form after the water evaporates, leaving the sediment minerals to crystallize and harden into rock.

We've already seen how evaporating salty seawater leaves behind salt and gypsum. But chemical sedimentary rocks can also form because of temperature changes and changes in the water's acid level. Such changes in water that contains a lot of calcium can leave calcium carbonate deposits, which over time build into limestone.

Limestone is a light-colored rock that normally forms in shallow and warm ocean waters. It can be formed by both chemical and organic processes. Seashells make up a large portion of organic limestone. Chemical limestone is made mostly of calcite.

Wherever we find limestone, we know that a lake or ocean once existed. Mount Everest sports a limestone peak, which tells us that millions of years ago, that peak was on an ocean floor.

Tufa is a type of chemical sedimentary rock that forms where calcium-filled underwater springs mix with lake water that contains a lot of carbonates. Carbonates are soft minerals made by metal, carbon, and oxygen. When the two waters mix, calcium carbonate, a type of limestone, forms. Over hundreds of years, the water evaporates, leaving the calcium carbonate to form underwater tufa towers. And with the passage of even more time, some of the tufa-filled lakes and springs dry up. Now these strangely shaped, otherworldly tufa towers are exposed for all of us to marvel over. These tufa towers are so remarkable that those of Trona Pinnacles in the Mojave Desert, in California, U.S.A., have been featured in science-fiction movies and TV shows. Pyramid Lake, in Nevada, U.S.A., and Mono Lake, in California, are two more places where you can see these tufa towers for yourself.

We've looked at the mineral halite, also known as table salt. But halite is also the name we give rock salt, a rock that is made up of halite crystals left behind by evaporating ocean water. Rock salt is found on Earth's surface only in very

THE TRONA PINNACLES IN THE MOJAVE DESERT ARE TUFA TOWERS.

WATER RUNOFF FROM MOUNTAINS IN THE DESERTS OF THE SOUTHWESTERN U.S.A. FORMS SHALLOW LAKES CALLED PLAYAS. WHEN THE SUMMER HEAT EVAPORATES THE WATER, HALITE (SALT) AND GYPSUM CRYSTALS ARE LEFT BEHIND. OVER THOUSANDS OF YEARS, THESE CRYSTALS GET PRESSED INTO CHEMICAL SEDIMENTARY ROCKS.

MANY **CAVES** ARE FORMED FROM LARGE **ROCKS CARVED UP** BY SLOW-MOVING **WATER.**

STALACTITES FORMED BY DRIPPING WATER AND MINERAL DEPOSITS

GRUTA DO LAGO AZUL, OR THE BLUE LAKE GROTTO, IN BONITO, BRAZIL

# STONE ICICLES

**CAVES SEEM LIKE ALIEN WORLDS** when you step into their dark, damp realms. But it's not surprising that caves feel damp. Most of them are carved out of rocks, such as limestone, by slow-moving groundwater.

Some of a cave's most alien-looking structures are stalactites and stalagmites. They're formed by rainwater and groundwater seeping through cracks in the ground. The water trickles through the limestone, dissolving and transporting minerals like calcite into the cave. The water drips from the cave's ceiling, leaving calcite behind. The calcite follows the form of the dripping water and creates a stone icicle called a stalactite. Any water that drips to the floor and still carries dissolved calcite forms an upside-down stalactite called a stalagmite. Both stalactites and stalagmites are made of the chemical sedimentary rocks limestone and travertine.

Some people have a hard time remembering which formation is a stalactite and which is a stalagmite. An easy way to keep them straight is to think of the *c* and *t* in "stalactite" as standing for "ceiling" and "top," and the *g* in "stalagmite" as standing for "ground."

dry regions and in old dried-up sea beds. More commonly, it's found underground, where it's mined to be used on icy roads to keep cars from sliding around. Rock salt is lighter, less dense, than the surrounding rock, so it can rise above the denser, heavier sedimentary rock to form salt domes.

The mineral gypsum also forms a chemical sedimentary rock in ocean waters. Gypsum crystals are deposited as the salt water evaporates, and then over time the crystals build up to form thick beds of gypsum rock.

In some cases, a type of rock can form as a chemical sedimentary rock and as an organic sedimentary rock, depending on its surroundings. Limestone, for instance, sometimes forms as the result of a chemical reaction or as the organic buildup of shells. But some sedimentary rocks are formed purely by the remains of living organisms. Let's take a look.

LIMESTONE EMBEDDED WITH FOSSILS OF SEA LILIES

## Organic Sedimentary Rocks

When plants and animals die, their remains lie on the ground or on the floor of bodies of water, such as oceans or lakes. Bones, shells, leaves, flower petals, skeletons, even materials produced by living things, such as dung and tree sap—they all contain carbon and hydrogen and are considered to be organic. As with any sedimentary rock, the organic matter piles up over thousands of years and gets compressed and cemented into sedimentary rock. With organic sedimentary rocks, the amount of pressure the organic material is under and its temperature determine what type of rock will be formed.

Did you know that in many parts of the world, the electricity used to turn on lights, watch TV, or play video games is fueled by a type of rock? It's coal, an organic sedimentary rock and the only rock that can burn. Coal is a nonrenewable natural resource. That means only a certain amount of it exists on Earth, so we need to be careful we don't use it all up.

Coal forms in swampy, acidic water in tropical, humid areas where a lot of plants grow. Over hundreds of thousands of years, plants die and pile up on the bottom of the still and swampy water. Oxygen is needed for decomposition to occur, but with all the dead plant parts, oxygen can't survive. So, very little of the plant material decays. This sludge of water and plant matter forms into peat. Peat is a rich, soil-like material made of decomposing plants. Over millions of years, sediment continues to be layered on top of the peat, compressing and heating the plant matter further until it hardens into coal.

Different types of coal are formed depending on the amount of heat and compression. For example, a brown coal called lignite forms as peat becomes more compressed. It's a soft rock, and since it's fairly young, you can still see some of the plant matter. As pressure and temperature increase, bituminous coal is formed. We use bituminous coal to generate electricity and heat. It's black and shiny, and you might be able to see its layers if you look closely.

Chalk is another organic sedimentary rock. Millions of years ago, the hard bones of tiny microscopic marine creatures covered the ocean floor. These

ELECTRICITY- AND HEAT-PRODUCING BITUMINOUS COAL

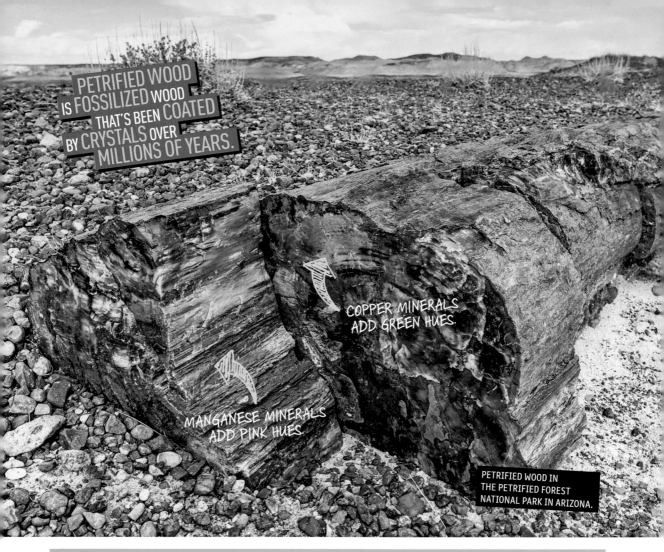

PETRIFIED WOOD IS FOSSILIZED WOOD THAT'S BEEN COATED BY CRYSTALS OVER MILLIONS OF YEARS.

COPPER MINERALS ADD GREEN HUES.

MANGANESE MINERALS ADD PINK HUES.

PETRIFIED WOOD IN THE PETRIFIED FOREST NATIONAL PARK IN ARIZONA.

## MAGIC WOOD

**IT'S HARD TO BELIEVE, BUT WOOD CAN BE TURNED TO STONE.** This "magic" of nature is called petrified wood. Here's the story:

Millions of years ago, trees died and fell to the ground. Some fell into streams or rivers and got carried downstream, tumbling with other sediment in the churning water. They floated through lakes and swamps, and eventually, they were stopped by mud and debris. Sometimes volcanic ash was among the mix. The wood got buried, and in time it started to decompose. Water, with its dissolved chemicals—including those from the volcanic ash—seeped into the decaying wood, eventually replacing it and forming mostly quartz crystals. Over millions of years, the wood became coated by crystals, and eventually, all that was left was a fossil. The original wood had been replaced by rock. And in many cases, the grain and bark texture of the original tree were preserved.

Petrified wood is harder than steel. It can be very colorful, all thanks to the dissolved minerals that seeped into the wood. Copper minerals, for instance, added green; manganese added pink.

hard bones became fossils when they got mixed into mud and hardened. Eventually, they formed the soft, light-colored limestone called chalk. Around 10,000 years ago, natural chalk was first used for writing and drawing. The chalk we use today, though, includes gypsum and is made in a factory.

Chert is a hard, glassy organic sedimentary rock that breaks with a conchoidal fracture (a fracture with a curved, smooth surface). It's made mostly of the mineral silica that can dissolve and recrystallize as tiny quartz crystals. Chert forms in seawater in layers and as nodules, or lumps. The silica comes from the shells and skeletons of tiny marine organisms that have drifted to the bottom of the ocean.

AN ARROWHEAD CARVED FROM FLINT

Flint is a type of chert that forms as nodules. It's extremely hard and breaks into sharp pieces. Two million years ago, people used flint to make pointy tools like arrowheads and spears.

## Metamorphic Rocks

Deep underground is where extreme pressure and heat change igneous and sedimentary rocks into metamorphic rocks. Pressure and heat can even transform metamorphic rocks into new metamorphic rocks, ones that are different from the originals. And all this can happen almost instantly, or it can take millions of years.

One way that metamorphic rocks form is through the action of tectonic plates sliding past one another or colliding into one another. This is how mountains and mountain ranges are formed. Friction between two plates creates pressure and heat high enough to melt rocks. At the point of impact, igneous and sedimentary rocks can be scraped into tiny bits and into powder and then re-formed as metamorphic rock.

Metamorphic rocks also form when rock contacts magma. Hot gases and fluids from magma force their way into a rock's pores and

# LAPIS LAZULI

**EVEN THOUGH YOU'LL SEE LAPIS FORMED INTO JEWELRY, IT'S NOT A GEMSTONE.** This metamorphic rock gets its striking blue color from the mineral lazurite. Some lapis contain pyrite, which adds gold flecks to the rock. Artists have used a brilliant ultramarine blue paint made from lapis lazuli for more than one thousand years. Vincent van Gogh's *The Starry Night* is one of the better-known paintings that wows us with its bright ultramarine color. Blue paint made with lapis lazuli became expensive, so now synthetic ultramarine is used.

LAPIS LAZULI GETS ITS BLUE HUE FROM LAZURITE.

VINCENT VAN GOGH'S *THE STARRY NIGHT* FEATURES A BRILLIANT BLUE THANKS TO LAPIS LAZULI.

create chemical reactions. Eventually, the rock's chemistry changes, creating a metamorphic rock.

When heat and pressure are high enough to melt rock into magma, some of the liquid escapes as steam. Minerals that had dissolved in the magma are also released with the steam. These minerals recrystallize, forming new minerals, which in turn form metamorphic rocks.

Scientists have divided metamorphic rocks into two categories: foliated rocks, which are banded, and nonfoliated, which are not banded. You can identify a foliated metamorphic rock by its swirled, twisted, or folded bands. But you can't identify a nonfoliated metamorphic rock just by its appearance. It can be identified only by its chemical makeup.

## Foliated Metamorphic Rocks

Foliated metamorphic rocks include slate, schist, and gneiss (pronounced like the word "nice"). They contain a lot of mica and chlorite minerals and tend to be banded, or striped. While they're forming, the pressure on these rocks is so strong that it forces their minerals to line up, against the pressure, so they look like they're made of plates or sheets. Foliated rocks are usually formed by the colliding of tectonic plates.

Slate is made when clay and silt get pressed by tectonic activity into shale and mudstone, which are sedimentary rocks. As the layers build, the pressure buries the shale and mudstone rocks deeper and deeper. The pressure and temperature increase until, after millions of years, mica minerals and slate are formed.

We use slate in a variety of ways. It was the first chalkboard used in schools, for example, and it's often used now as flooring and roofing.

Compared to other metamorphic rocks, slate forms at fairly low pressures and temperatures. As both pressure and temperature increase, though, a glossy rock called phyllite is formed. Add even more pressure and heat, and you have a flaky rock called schist.

When schist is put under more heat and pressure, a banded metamorphic rock called gneiss is formed. The alternating dark and light

GNEISS AT THE BUTT OF LEWIS IN SCOTLAND, U.K., IS SOME OF THE OLDEST IN THE WORLD, ESTIMATED TO BE AT LEAST 3 BILLION YEARS OLD.

SLATE HAS LOTS OF USES— INCLUDING AS ROOF TILES. IT WEATHERS WELL AND CAN LAST A LONG TIME.

stripes in gneiss reflect the layering of different minerals, including feldspar, quartz, and mica. The clay in schist changes to sheets of mica, which then get bigger and recrystallize into the coarse-grained gneiss. Gneiss is often found as part of mountain ranges and can form from either sedimentary or igneous rocks.

## Nonfoliated Metamorphic Rocks

Nonfoliated metamorphic rocks include marble, quartzite, and anthracite. They are often formed where the pressures are low and equal in all directions, and the temperatures are high. Pressures may force the rock to become denser and the minerals to recrystallize and form larger crystals, or new crystals may be introduced that cause recrystallization.

Marble is a nonfoliated metamorphic rock that's made mostly of the mineral calcite. Basically, it's limestone pressed and heated into its metamorphic form of marble. The calcite in limestone comes from fossilized shells and other organic matter. As it changes into marble, limestone's small crystals grow and recrystallize, altering the texture of the rock.

Quartzite forms when sandstone made mostly of the mineral quartz mixes with magma deep underground. This happens mostly as mountains are being built through the movement of tectonic plates. Quartzite ends up looking a lot like its parent sedimentary rock, sandstone, but quartzite is a lot harder, ranking a 7 on the Mohs scale of hardness. It's so hard that it often holds up to weathering that sweeps away other, less durable rocks. Ancient peoples used quartzite to make knife blades and ax heads. Today, we use quartzite as countertops, flooring, and roofing tiles.

What happens when shale or mudstone gets mixed up with magma? You get a nonfoliated metamorphic rock called hornfels. This is a pretty drab rock with nothing striking to distinguish it from other rocks. At least not until you take a look at it under a microscope. Then you see that hornfels contains fine-grained minerals of about equal size that fit together like puzzle pieces. The minerals inside can be a variety, including everything from pyrite to biotite. Hornfels is such a hard rock that prehistoric people made arrowheads and knives with it. Today, we use hornfels in many ways, including as a building material, in paving stones, and in concrete.

A CLOSE-UP OF A CROSS SECTION OF HORNFELS SHOWS THE BITS OF OTHER MINERALS THAT MAKE UP THIS ROCK. ANDALUSITE IS RED AGAINST THE OTHER SILICATES.

THE STATUE OF ABRAHAM LINCOLN AT THE LINCOLN MEMORIAL IN WASHINGTON, D.C., U.S.A, IS MADE OF 28 PIECES OF MARBLE FROM THE STATE OF GEORGIA.

# Out-of-This-World Rocks

Have you ever seen a nighttime light show of shooting stars and comets? Do you know that rocks are actually performing some of these out-of-this-world displays? Comets have a rocky, icy core that releases gas and dust. Scientists used to refer to them as dirty snowballs, but they've discovered that a better description of them is snowy dirt balls. Comets are famous for their dust-and-gas tails that streak across the sky. We can see the glow of a comet's tail only when it orbits close enough to the sun to reflect the sun's light.

Rocky, metallic asteroids also orbit the sun. They are oddly shaped and can be as small as a pebble or have a diameter of more than 600 miles (965 km). Asteroids sometimes speed toward Earth and experience changes along the way. We have different names for them depending on where they are during their trip to Earth. *Meteoroid* is the name we give an asteroid as it plunges toward Earth. When it hits Earth's atmosphere, some or all of it burns, creating a light trail that we call a meteor. We also call this a shooting star. If the meteor doesn't burn up completely, it crashes to Earth as a meteorite.

Some stone meteorites have chondrules, or small, round grains that formed in the solar nebula 4.6 billion years ago, making meteorites the oldest matter on Earth. When these extra-terrestrial rocks punch into Earth at thousands of miles (km) per hour, they create impact pits if they're small or craters if they're big. Meteorites can range from being the size of pebbles and baseballs to being as big as a building. Three main varieties of meteorites have crashed into Earth: iron, stony, and stony-iron.

Iron meteorites started life millions of years ago as part of the core of a planet or asteroid. They are one of the densest materials you can find on Earth, and they're not very common. They are up to 95 percent iron, and the rest is nickel and bits of other elements. Because of their iron content, they are attracted to magnets.

Stony meteorites are up to 90 percent silicon and contain some iron, so they also stick to magnets. These are the most common space rock found on Earth, but they were once the surface, or crust, of asteroids. They are often mistaken for common Earth rocks, but most show signs of being burned. Some stony meteorites are called chondrites because they contain chondrules, tiny colorful grains that are more than 4.6 billion years old—older than our solar system.

Stony-iron meteorites are basically an equal mix of stone and nickel-iron. They are the least common meteorite found on Earth, but two types have found their way here. One type, pallasites, are made mostly of the mineral olivine, giving them a greenish color. Peridot is the gemstone version of olivine, so when you polish a pallasite, the green gem shines. The other type, meso-siderites, are nearly half metal and half silicates made mostly of igneous rock. They are extremely rare on Earth, with fewer than 200 having been found.

It's exciting to think of space rocks on Earth, but meteorites give us more than just a thrill. We study what meteorites are made of and also determine their age, which help us unravel the history of Earth and our solar system.

STONY-IRON METEORITES CONTAIN A MIX OF ROCK AND NICKEL-IRON, AND THEY'RE VERY RARE ON EARTH.

# METEORITE STARS

**METEORITES HAVE AFFECTED EARTH IN SOME AMAZING WAYS.** Here are just a few examples of how outer space rocks have impacted Earth.

On February 15, 2013, eyes were focused on an **ASTEROID** named 2012 DA14. It was traveling dangerously close to Earth, about 17,200 miles (27,680 km) away. At 9:20 a.m., moving in the opposite direction of 2012 DA14, a large, bright unidentified flying object (UFO) fell from the sky and exploded about 15 miles (24 km) above Chelyabinsk, Russia. Scientists say the explosion was 30 to 40 times stronger than an atom bomb and brighter than the sun for at least a moment. Three days later, the first meteorite was found 43 miles (69 km) outside Chelyabinsk.

THE TRAIL OF THE UFO FLYING ON THE SAME MORNING AS 2012 DA14. THE TRAIL MIGHT HAVE COME FROM A METEORITE LATER FOUND NEAR CHELYABINSK, RUSSIA.

THE HOBA METEORITE NEAR GROOTFONTEIN, NAMIBIA

The biggest meteorite to hit Earth is **HOBA**, and it was found in Namibia in 1920. It landed about 80,000 years ago and weighs 66 tons (60 t). Namibia declared the site a national monument.

THE WILLAMETTE METEORITE IN THE AMERICAN MUSEUM OF NATURAL HISTORY IN NEW YORK CITY.

The **WILLAMETTE METEORITE** found in Oregon, U.S.A., is the largest meteorite in the United States and the sixth largest in the world. This iron meteorite hit Earth around 13,000 years ago and weighs 15 tons (14 t). You can see it today at the American Museum of Natural History in New York City.

**CHICXULUB CRATER** on the Yucatán Peninsula of Mexico is the result of a large asteroid smacking into Earth around 66 million years ago. The asteroid was so big that it left a crater more than 100 miles (160 km) wide. It's most noted for being the likely cause of the extinction of dinosaurs and 75 percent of the other animals that lived on Earth at the time. The impact of the asteroid that created the Chicxulub crater was equal in energy to 100 million atomic bombs!

AN ARTIST'S DEPICTION OF THE IMPACT AS THE CHICXULUB ASTEROID CRASHED TO EARTH

THE BARRINGER METEORITE CRATER, ALSO KNOWN AS METEOR CRATER TO VISITORS, IN ARIZONA, U.S.A.

Around 50,000 years ago, an iron meteorite about 150 feet (45 m) wide crash-landed in what's now northern Arizona at a speed of 26,000 miles an hour (42,000 km/h). Named the **BARRINGER METEORITE CRATER**, it's one of the best preserved craters on Earth. It's believed the meteorite was vaporized by its impact on Earth, so you won't find any good-size meteorites around the crater. But you will find meteorite bits and pieces scattered about.

# ROCK OUT!

**Here is a simple experiment to help you see how sedimentary rocks form.** Please make sure to get the help of a trusted adult as you conduct this experiment. Have fun making your own version of clastic and nonclastic sedimentary rocks!

CHERT, A NONCLASTIC SEDIMENTARY ROCK

CONGLOMERATE, A CLASTIC SEDIMENTARY ROCK

## What you need:

1 pen

3 large paper cups

¼ cup pea gravel

¼ cup sand

¼ cup topsoil

¼ cup small seashell bits (optional)

1 cup water

3 tbsp Elmer's glue or equivalent

¼ CUP TOPSOIL

PEN

3 LARGE PAPER CUPS

3 TBSP GLUE

# How to make your rocks:

Cup 1 (with the holes) will always be the middle cup; you will swap cup 2 and cup 3 throughout the activity.

1. **Use a pen to label each cup:** 1, 2, and 3.

2. **Have an adult help you poke holes in the bottom of cup 1,** using the tip of a sharp pencil or pen point. Make sure the holes are small enough so that sand won't pour through them.

3. **Add** the pea gravel, sand, and topsoil (and shells if you're using them) to cup 1.

4. **In cup 2,** mix together the water and glue.

5. **Hold cup 1 over cup 3, the empty paper cup.** Slowly pour the glue-and-water solution in cup 2 over the sediment in cup 1 so it drips through the holes into cup 3. Now cup 2 is empty and cup 3 holds the solution.

6. **Hold cup 1 over cup 2,** and slowly pour cup 3's solution over cup 1's sediment so it drips through the holes into cup 2. Repeat this at least five to six more times.

7. **During the last round,** hold the sediment-filled cup 1 over the glue-and-water-filled cup 2 until it's done dripping. This should take a few minutes.

8. **Place the sediment-filled cup 1 into the empty cup 3,** and set it and the glue-and-water-filled cup aside. Allow them to dry for two to four days.

9. **When the glue has dried completely,** tear or cut the paper cups away from the glue and the sediment. The sediment mixture is an example of clastic sedimentary rock; note the layers of sediment. The hardened glue-and-water solution is an example of nonclastic sedimentary rock. Describe the differences and the similarities between the two types of rocks.

2

1
(HAS HOLES)

3

THE GIZA PYRAMIDS IN CAIRO, EGYPT, DATE BACK TO 2600 B.C. AND WERE BUILT WITH IGNEOUS GRANITE AND SEDIMENTARY LIMESTONE.

# CHAPTER 4

# LIVING WITH ROCKS AND MINERALS

## IT'S NOT ALL ROCKS ALL THE TIME WHEN I'M DOING RESEARCH.

When my team and I are working in some places, like in Kenya, Africa, we often make trades with the community.

**DR. SARAH STAMPS**

We offer something that the community needs in exchange for a safe and secure place to set up our stations. During one trip to Kenya, my team and I found the bedrock we needed for our research. We thought it was perfect because it was also secure in a protected area.

The area was in the Ol Pejeta Conservancy. Rare animals such as the last white rhinos are protected there, and tourists are allowed in the conservancy to view them.

It was a perfect spot except for one thing: the animals. We'd have to worry about elephants trampling our equipment or baboons pushing it over. Our equipment wouldn't be safe there. So we were sent to look at a farm.

We found great rock on this farm, too. It was deep, it was solid, it was perfect. But, again, animals got in our way. This time it was elephants and a leopard that could cause damage. Our equipment is so tall that we were actually afraid the leopard would use it as a scratching post!

That evening, the people who owned the farm invited us in for tea and a special thin, crispy bread that's made locally. They told us about their water shortage. They weren't getting the rain they needed, so the whole area was dry. The geophysicist we were with offered to do a free survey to figure out the best place to drill for water, which means finding the locations of rocks that align with a fault. Then he would reach out to investors who would donate money for the drilling.

Even though the farm wasn't right for us because of the possibility of animals damaging our equipment, we were happy that we were able to help these kind people.

Whenever we find a place that has the perfect rocks for our measurements, we start negotiating with whoever owns that property so we can give back to them. Those rocks are very important to our work, so we have to strike a deal that allows us to keep our equipment there securely.

In the past, we have arranged for a high school's broken solar power system to be fixed and a water tank for a girls' dormitory to be installed. In one case, we even arranged for toilets to be built.

DR. STAMPS'S SPECIAL EQUIPMENT FIXED INTO BEDROCK IN OL PEJETA CONSERVANCY IN KENYA

IT CAN BE HARD TO FIND THE PERFECT PLACE TO SET UP VALUABLE RESEARCH EQUIPMENT—ESPECIALLY IN AREAS WHERE ELEPHANTS, RHINOS, AND LEOPARDS CAN TRAMPLE IT.

THE WHITE RHINOS OF OL PEJETA CONSERVANCY IN KENYA, AFRICA

OL PEJETA IS HOME TO 30 SOUTHERN WHITE RHINOS AND TWO OF THE LAST NORTHERN WHITE RHINOS.

# STOP AND TAKE A MOMENT TO LOOK AT THE WORLD AROUND YOU.

**Even if you don't see actual rocks or minerals, everywhere you turn you'll see one being used in some way.**

Do you see a computer? It probably has copper wiring and uses silver and quartz in its electronics. Your pencil is made of graphite, concrete sidewalks contain gravel and sand, and scissors are made of iron and nickel. Even your lunch contains minerals—but not rocks! Let's take a look at all the ways rocks and minerals are used in our everyday lives.

## Arty Buildings and Building Art

Many structures we live, play, and work in are built with brick, which is made of clay. And clay is a combination of minerals, including a mix of silicon, oxygen, and aluminum called aluminum silicate. You can find granite, soapstone, and quartz countertops in many homes. Marble, slate, and a red clay called terra-cotta cover the floors of many homes and businesses. Bridges can be made of granite, limestone, concrete, or steel, which comes from minerals, including the iron ores hematite and magnetite.

Rocks and minerals are also used to make glass (which contains quartz sand), drywall (which contains gypsum), and the framework of skyscrapers (a mix of iron and carbon called steel). Many minerals go into making house paints, including calcium carbonate, clay, talc, and zinc oxide.

Speaking of paint, rocks and minerals are used a lot in art—from prehistoric cave paintings that date back 65,000 years to today. Black and a shade of red called ochre were the main colors used by ancient peoples to paint stories on cave walls. Red ochre was made from the mineral hematite (iron oxide, which is a mix of iron and oxygen), and black was made from charcoal and

COPPER WIRING INSIDE A COMPUTER

manganese dioxide (a compound made of manganese and oxygen).

When people started painting on canvases, paint colors were made from different types of powdered minerals or rocks mixed with wax or animal fat. Here are some examples:

- Azurite: Blue
- Cinnabar: Vermilion (reddish orange)
- Coal: Black
- Diatomite: White
- Hematite: Red
- Lapis lazuli: Dark blue
- Malachite: Green
- Limonite: Yellow

Many paints made of minerals are toxic, so today, colors are often made of synthetic materials made by people.

Paints aren't the only way rocks and minerals have made an impact on the art world. Since ancient times, artists have carved detailed, lifelike statues out of stone. Marble is easy to carve, and depending on its mineral

impurities, or other bits of elements, it can be found in shades of black, brown, gray, green, pink, or white. Michelangelo's statue *David* is an example of how realistic marble statues can be in the hands of a skilled and creative artist.

Limestone, the sedimentary and softer version of marble, is also used for carving statues.

Standing on Easter Island, also called Rapa Nui, a volcanic island in the southeastern Pacific Ocean, are about 900 statues. On average, they stand 13 feet (4 m) high and weigh 14 tons (13 t).

These moai, known as the heads of Easter Island, were carved between A.D. 1100 and the mid-17th century out of tuff. Recently, scientists have discovered that the heads of Easter Island actually have bodies, too! They believe the bodies were buried naturally by dirt over hundreds of years. No one knows

MICHELANGELO'S *DAVID*, LOCATED IN ITALY, IS A STATUE SCULPTED FROM MARBLE.

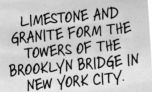
LIMESTONE AND GRANITE FORM THE TOWERS OF THE BROOKLYN BRIDGE IN NEW YORK CITY.

EASTER ISLAND STATUES ARE MADE FROM TUFF.

THE MAJESTIC **TAJ MAHAL** IN INDIA IS MADE FROM **METAMORPHIC** ROCK—**WHITE MARBLE,** TO BE EXACT.

THE TAJ MAHAL IN AGRA, INDIA

# STONY STRUCTURES

**PEOPLE HAVE BEEN BUILDING WITH ROCK SINCE ANCIENT TIMES.** Egyptian sculptures and buildings made from rock date back to 2600 B.C. The Egyptian pyramids were built with igneous granite and sedimentary limestone. The tallest of these structures reaches up to 204 feet (62 m). The Taj Mahal in India is a metamorphic white-marble masterpiece that some say took 20,000 people and 1,000 elephants to build. Marble isn't the only rock in the Taj Mahal. Precious stones like lapis lazuli and amethyst decorate the interior. Building began in 1632 and continued for about 20 years. At its tallest point, the Taj Mahal is 240 feet (73 m). Both the pyramids and the Taj Mahal were built as memorials—the pyramids for pharaohs who passed away, and the Taj Mahal for an empress.

for certain why these statues were created. The Rapa Nui, the ancient peoples who lived on the island, left no written explanation. And the culture became extinct, so any oral stories behind the sculptures' creation have been lost.

The most familiar decorative use of rocks and minerals is probably in the jewelry we wear. Many rocks and minerals, such as diamonds, garnets, gold, silver, and emeralds, take on sparkle and shine when they are cut and polished. From ancient times, people have enjoyed finding ways to wrap shiny, colorful, sparkling gemstones around finger, wrist, and neck.

CALCIUM IN FOOD AND DRINKS SUCH AS MILK HELP BUILD HEALTHY BONES AND TEETH.

## Growing Strong and Healthy With Minerals

So far we've looked at the rocks and minerals that are all around us, but we also need minerals to keep our bodies healthy. Minerals find ways into our bodies through the water we drink and the foods we eat. Without these minerals, we would not thrive.

Most of the minerals we need to stay healthy can be found on Earth's crust. But obviously, it wouldn't do us any good to eat the soil and rocks that make up the crust, and it wouldn't be very tasty. Instead, weathering and erosion break rocks down so their minerals become part of the soil. Plants draw up water, minerals, and other nutrients from the soil through their roots. Animals eat the plants, including the minerals stored in them. So by eating plants directly or by eating other animals that have eaten plants, we're getting the minerals we need to stay healthy.

Why do we need minerals? Well, without minerals, you'd be flopping around, and you wouldn't be able to bite into your food. That's because calcium helps build bones and teeth. Without magnesium and potassium, your nerves and muscles wouldn't function properly. Iron is part of a substance in your red blood cells that carries oxygen through your whole body. And zinc keeps your immune system working so

FREE-RANGE CHICKENS GET NUTRIENTS FROM THE GRASS THEY EAT, WHICH IN TURN GETS ITS NUTRIENTS FROM THE EARTH.

VEGETABLES, INCLUDING CARROTS, GET MINERALS AND NUTRIENTS FROM THE SOIL THEY'RE PLANTED IN.

# MERCURY GOT THE MAD HATTER

**SOME MINERALS CAN BE HARMFUL TO US.** Mercury is one of those minerals. In the mid-1800s, British hatmakers soaked wool felt in a mercury solution called mercuric nitrate, and then shaped the felt into hats. Day after day, the hatmakers breathed in the vapors of this toxic brew. After a while, it began affecting their health. They began twitching and drooling and acting strange. So it came to be that when someone acted crazy, people would say he was mad as a hatter.

During that time, Lewis Carroll was writing *Alice's Adventures in Wonderland*. Many think that the Mad Hatter character was based on this newly discovered effect of mercury. Mercury was finally banned in felt manufacturing in the United States in 1941.

MERCURY IS IN LIQUID FORM AT ROOM TEMPERATURE.

your body can fight off sickness. These are just a few of the minerals we rely on for good health.

The utensils we use to eat our mineral-rich food are themselves made of minerals. Most of us use stainless-steel forks and knives, which are made mostly of iron and chromium. And if you want to get really fancy, you can eat with utensils made of silver or copper.

Minerals are not only in the food we eat but also in the supplements we may take. Some people start off their day by taking vitamin and mineral pills. Usually, though, you can get all the vitamins and minerals you need by eating a variety of healthy foods.

We take advantage of minerals for other medical needs. When adults get an upset stomach, they may chew a calcium carbonate (chalk) tablet to get rid of the heartburn. Silver is used in antibiotic creams and some bandages because it aids healing and keeps bacteria from growing. Copper kills viruses, bacteria, and fungi, so hospitals have started using copper-infused bed linens and gowns, as well as copper bedrails and sinks. The list of benefits could go on and on.

## Tools and Technology

We've made most of our tools from rocks and minerals. It started about 2.5 million years ago, when rocks were used as hammers to chip away at other stones. They are called hammerstones and were used to break nuts and animal bones and crush seeds and clay. The crushed clay was used to make pigments. Hammerstones were also used to chip away at other rocks to make early knives and digging tools. Today, many of our tools are complex

A DIAMOND-COATED SAW BLADE IS EXTRA STRONG AND CAN CUT THROUGH HARD ROCK.

steel machines made of iron and carbon. Diamond, one of the hardest materials on Earth, is used as part of cutting and drilling tools in many industries. For example, diamond-coated saw blades are used for cutting hard rock. Sandpaper is made of aluminum oxide or, believe it or not, the gemstone garnet.

Rocks and minerals are no stranger to technology, either. Quartz crystals, for instance, help watches and clocks tick, but they're also used in electronic games, TVs, cell phones, computers, and GPS devices, among other uses. Barium is used in x-rays, copper conducts electricity and is often used as

SANDPAPER MADE FROM ALUMINUM OXIDE

wiring, and graphite and lithium are used in batteries. Pretty much any time you press a button, turn a knob, or click on something, rocks or minerals are involved in some way.

Technology has found its way into our homes, and so have rocks and minerals. Along with granite countertops and gypsum drywall, the element tungsten from the minerals scheelite and wolframite is used in light bulbs. Your bathtubs, toilets, and sinks are likely made of porcelain, which is a mix of feldspar, kaolin, and quartz.

In every room of your house, you'll find items that had their beginnings as rocks or minerals.

# ROCK
# OUT!

**ROCK PAINT!**

For centuries, people have been making their own paint from rocks, and you can too! All it takes are some rock-hunting skills and a little elbow grease.

Before you get started, you need to find your rocks. Look for soft rocks—sandstone with its tiny grains is a good choice—and pick up the most colorful ones. You can use your fingernail to try to scrape powder off the rocks to determine if they're soft. Choose rocks that fit in your hand. These will be the easiest to work with.

EXAMPLES OF SANDSTONE ROCKS

## What to do with your rocks:

1. **Once you get home, rinse your rocks with water, and then let them dry.** If your rocks are very soft, you can rub them together over a plate or bowl and watch as powder scrapes off of them. Do this for as long as needed to get the amount of pigment you want. If your rocks are too hard to scrape, then go on to step 2.

SAFETY GOGGLES

2. **Ask an adult to help you with this step, and wear safety goggles.** You may want to do this outside. Use a mortar and pestle to grind your rocks into a fine powder. This will take some time. You can add a bit of water to keep dust from flying everywhere. If you don't have a mortar and pestle, place your rocks on top of an old towel, fold the towel over the rocks, and then ask an adult to help you pound them into a powder with a hammer. The finer the powder, the smoother your paint will be.

HAMMER

3. **Add water to the powder, little by little, until it's the consistency of paint.** The less water you use, the more vibrant the color will be. Now you're ready to paint your masterpiece!

MORTAR AND PESTLE

TOWEL (OPTIONAL)

WATER

Water acts like a binder, turning the powder from your rocks into liquid paint. But other substances can be used as binders, and they give paint different intensities of color and depth. Some of the binders people use to make their own paint include flaxseed oil, which was used a lot around the 17th century; egg yolk, which makes a permanent paint that dries quickly; and beeswax, which was used by the ancient Greeks.

# GLOSSARY

**ACID RAIN:** Rain made more acid by pollutants in the air

**AGGREGATE:** A mass made up of bits of rock or minerals or both

**ARID:** Very dry

**ASTHENOSPHERE:** An area below the lithosphere in the upper mantle, where rock is partially melted

**ATOM:** A basic unit of matter; the smallest part of an element that can exist either alone or in combination with other elements

**BITUMINOUS COAL:** A dark, banded sedimentary rock that is most often used as fuel to generate energy

**BLADED:** Elongated and flattened crystal

**BRITTLE:** Breakable or can shatter into a powder easily

**CALCITE:** One of the three subgroups of carbonate minerals, or a mineral with the chemical formula $CaCO_3$

**CARBONATE:** A mineral made of a combination of carbon, oxygen, and one or more metallic or semimetallic elements

**CHALK:** A soft, light-colored limestone

**CLASTIC:** Made up of fragments of preexisting minerals and rocks

**CLEAVAGE:** A weakness along the flat surface of a crystal structure along which a mineral breaks

**COLOR:** A property used in identifying a mineral

**COLUMNAR:** A crystal structure made of separate, often parallel columns

**CONCHOIDAL:** Shaped like a scallop shell, smooth and rounded

**CONGLOMERATE:** A clastic sedimentary rock made of rounded pebbles that are cemented together by grains of a quartz-and-calcite glue

**CONVERGENT PLATE BOUNDARY:** A boundary between two tectonic plates that are moving toward each other

**CORE:** The innermost part of Earth, divided into the inner solid core and the outer liquid core

**CRUST:** The rocky uppermost part of Earth that supports life, including the rocky upper mantle and lower mantle

**CRYSTAL:** A natural solid substance that has atoms arranged in an ordered three-dimensional pattern

**CUBE:** A crystal form made of six faces of equal size that's shaped similar to a playing die

**DEBRIS:** The remains of something that has broken down or was destroyed

**DECOMPOSE:** To rot or break down into parts

**DENSE:** A rock or mineral with tightly packed atoms, making it heavy for its size

**DEPOSIT:** A natural accumulation

**ELECTRON:** A tiny negatively charged particle that moves around an atom's nucleus

**ELEMENT:** A substance that can't be chemically broken down into smaller parts; each element is identified by the number of protons it has.

**EROSION:** The process that moves sediment from one place to another

**EXTRUSIVE ROCK:** An igneous rock that forms when magma rises to Earth's surface through a volcano and cools quickly.

**FACE:** Flat surface of a crystal; also called a plane

**FAULT:** A long break or crack in Earth's crust

**FELDSPAR:** A group of common silicate minerals, which help form rocks and are found in igneous, metamorphic, and sedimentary rocks; feldspar makes up more than half of Earth's crust.

**FELSIC:** Lightweight, light-colored rocks that are made mostly of silicon- and aluminum-rich minerals

**FIBROUS:** A mineral habit, or shape, made of thin threadlike strands

**FLUORESCENT:** Glow-in-the-dark light that is seen when exposed to ultraviolet radiation

**FOLIATED:** Rocks that form thin sheetlike layers

**FRACTURE:** The way a mineral breaks or chips that is different from its cleavage

**GLASSY:** Igneous rocks that cool too quickly for crystals to form, causing their surfaces to be smooth and shiny like glass

**GRAIN:** A rock or mineral particle smaller than a few millimeters in diameter; a way to describe rock texture, for example, fine-grained

**HABIT:** The shape of a mineral's crystal, which is often the same shape as its lattice

**HARDNESS:** How resistant a mineral is to being scratched

**IGNEOUS:** A type of rock formed by the cooling and solidifying of hot magma and lava

**IMPURITY:** An element mixed into a mineral's crystal that's not part of the mineral's natural makeup; an impurity can affect a mineral's color.

**INTRUSIVE ROCK:** A rough-textured igneous rock with large crystals that forms slowly underground as magma cools; also called plutonic

**ISOMETRIC:** One of the seven crystal lattice shapes, or systems; the crystal is in the shape of a cube.

**LATTICE:** The pattern atoms form in a crystal.

**LAVA:** Hot, molten rock that has reached Earth's surface

**LITHOSPHERE:** The outer part of Earth, including the crust and upper mantle lithosphere

**LUSTER:** The way light reflects off a mineral's surface; a mineral's shininess; one of the ways to identify minerals

**MAFIC:** Heavy, dark-colored rocks that are made mostly of magnesium- and iron-rich minerals

**MAGMA:** Hot, molten rock that is below or within Earth's crust

**MANTLE:** The biggest layer of Earth between the base of the crust and the top of the core; divided into the upper and the lower mantle

**MATTER:** Any type of material

**METALLIC:** Minerals that are shiny like metals, such as gold

**METALLOID:** See semimetal

**METAMORPHIC:** A rock created by heat and immense pressure deep within Earth that causes new minerals to form

DETAILED PATTERNS FORM IN A LACE AGATE GEODE; AGATE IS A TYPE OF QUARTZ.

**METEOR:** A piece of rock or metal that burns and glows as it falls from space into Earth's atmosphere; also called a shooting star

**METEORITE:** A meteor that does not burn up before it crashes into Earth

**METEOROID:** An asteroid that is plunging toward Earth

**MOLECULE:** Two or more atoms that have bonded together

**NATIVE ELEMENTS:** Minerals made of only one kind of atom; divided into metals, semimetals, and nonmetals

**NEUTRON:** A tiny particle that has no electrical charge that is in the nucleus of every atom except hydrogen atoms

**NUCLEUS:** The central part of an atom that is made up of protons and neutrons

**OCTAHEDRAL:** A crystal form having eight triangular planes in four directions

**OPAQUE:** Not transparent; a substance that doesn't let light pass through it

**ORE:** A rock or mineral containing something valuable, such as a metal, that can be mined for a profit

**ORGANIC:** Made up of materials that were once alive or are from a living being

**ORTHORHOMBIC:** One of the seven crystal lattice shapes, or systems, with three unequal axes that are at right angles to one another

**PERIODIC TABLE:** A table where all the elements are arranged by their atomic number

**PETRIFY:** To become stone

**PLAGIOCLASE:** One of two groups of feldspars that contain calcium and sodium

**PLATE TECTONICS:** A theory that the lithosphere, or outer part of Earth, is divided into plates that move, causing earthquakes, building mountains, and otherwise changing the shape of Earth's surface.

**PLUTONIC:** See intrusive

**POROUS:** Being full of pores, cells, and other spaces that may or may not interconnect

**PRIMARY MINERAL:** A mineral that forms from cooling magma

**PROPERTY:** A physical or chemical characteristic of a material

**PROTON:** A tiny positively charged particle in the nucleus of every atom

**RIFT VALLEY:** A low area of land between hills or mountains that's caused by Earth's crust spreading apart

**SECONDARY MINERAL:** A mineral that forms near or at Earth's surface from bits of weathered primary minerals

**SEDIMENT:** Fragments of rocks and minerals, as well as animal and plant material

**SEDIMENTARY:** A rock formed by piled-up sediment that was cemented together

**SEMIMETAL:** A native element with characteristics that fall between those of the metallic and the nonmetallic elements; also called metalloid

**SILT:** Loose sedimentary material containing tiny rock particles

**SPECIFIC GRAVITY:** A measurement of a mineral's weight as it compares to an equal volume of water

**STALACTITE:** A cone- or icicle-shaped mineral deposit that hangs from a cave's ceiling

**STALAGMITE:** A cone- or icicle-shaped mineral deposit that forms on a cave's floor

**STREAK:** The color of a mineral's powder

**STREAK PLATE:** The white unglazed porcelain tile used to scrape a mineral across to determine its streak

**SYSTEMS:** The seven basic lattice shapes in crystals

**TABULAR:** A crystal that looks like a paper tablet

**TECTONIC PLATE:** One of the giant slabs of Earth's lithosphere that moves and bumps into other plates, causing earthquakes and volcanoes

**TETRAGONAL:** One of the seven crystal lattice shapes, or systems; looks like a rectangular cube with a prism and square base

**TETRAHEDRON:** A triangular pyramid shape; this is the shape that four oxygen atoms form around one silicon atom in a silicate, for example. The arrangement of a tetrahedron in a silicate determines the subgroup

**TRANSPARENT:** An object that's clear enough that you can see through it

**VOLCANO:** An opening in Earth's surface that allows molten rock and gases to escape

**WEATHERING:** The slow process of rocks crumbling into sediment as a result of exposure to weather, such as rain and wind

# FOR MORE ROCKS AND MINERALS READING, CHECK OUT:

Honovich, Nancy. *National Geographic Kids Ultimate Explorer Field Guide: Rocks and Minerals.* National Geographic Kids Books, 2016.

Tomecek, Stephen M. *National Geographic Kids Dirtmeister's Nitty Gritty Planet Earth.* National Geographic Kids Books, 2016.

Tomecek, Stephen M. *National Geographic Kids Everything Rocks and Minerals.* National Geographic Kids Books, 2011.

**NATIONAL GEOGRAPHIC KIDS: GEOLOGY 101 WEBSITE** kids.nationalgeographic.com/explore/science/geology-101

**GEOLOGY.COM WEBSITE** geology.com

**U.S. GEOLOGICAL SURVEY: MINERAL RESOURCES PROGRAM WEBSITE** minerals.usgs.gov

# INDEX

**Boldface** indicates photos or illustrations.

## A

Activities
  crystal candy 64–65, **64–65**
  make your own volcano 28–29, **28–29**
  rock paint 104–105, **104–105**
  sedimentary cementing 92–93, **92–93**
Adamite 59, **59**
Agate **30–31, 107**
Alexandrite **62–63**
Amber 25, **25,** 61
Amethyst **35, 36,** 61, **63,** 100
Andesite 76
Antimony 49, **49,** 50
Aquamarine 60, **63,** 73
Aragonite 54, 55
Asteroids 12, 89, 90, 91, **91**
Asthenosphere 14, 17, 19, 23
Atoms 22, 34, 46–47
Azurite 39, 41, 54
Azurmalachite 54, **54**

## B

Barite 39, 40, 56, **56**
Basalt 21, 72–73, 74, 75
  close-up **74**
  columnar **66–67,** 71, **71**
Bedrock 7, 69, 96, **97**
Biotite 41, 72, **72**
Birthstones 62–63, **62–63**
Black sand 14, **14**
Breccia 80, 81, **81**

## C

Calcite **45,** 55
  on faucets 79, **79**
  fluorescence **59**
  hardness test **44, 45**
  stone icicles 83, **83**
Calcium: in food and drinks 37, 101
Calcium carbonate 55, 82, 98, 102
Carbonates 48, 54–55
Caves 36, 83, **83,** 98
Celestite **36,** 39
Chalk 84, 86, 102
Chert 86, **92**
Cinder cone volcanoes 21, **21**
Cinnabar 41, 51, **51,** 53, 99
Coal 25, **25,** 84, **84,** 99
Comets 12, 89
Composite volcanoes 21, **21,** 76
Conglomerate 79, 80, 81, **81, 92**
Copper
  float copper 49, **49**
  mines 32, 52, **52**
  ores 52, 54, **54–55**
  uses 22, 39, 49, 98, **98,** 102, 103
Corundum **38,** 45, **45,** 73
Crystals
  experiment 64–65, **64–65**
  geodes 36, **36,** 59, 61
  habits 34
  lattice shapes 34, **35**
  and minerals 37

## D

Dana, James Dwight 48, **48**
Dead Sea 58, **58**
Diamonds
  cut and polished **46, 62,** 101
  formation 34, 37, 74
  properties 37, 40, 44, 45
  in the rough **74**
  uses 101, 103
Diatomite 99
Dolomite 42, **42,** 54, 55

## E

Earth (planet)
  formation 13
  layers 13–18, **16**
  magnetic field 14, 15
  plate tectonics 18–19, 26–27, **27,** 68
  space-rock impacts 89, 90, 91, **91**
Earthquakes 7, 10, 17, 18, 19, 27, 32
Easter Island, South Pacific Ocean 99, **99,** 101
Egypt, ancient 49, **49,** 53, **94–95,** 100
Elements, periodic table of 46–47, **46–47**
Emeralds 61, **61, 62,** 101
Empress of Uruguay (geode) 36, **36**
Everest, Mount, China-Nepal 19, **19,** 82

## F

Feldspar 16, 18, **45,** 72, **72**
Fireworks 36, 39, **39,** 50
Flint 61, 86, **86**
Fluorescence 58–59, **59**
Fluorite 42, **42, 45, 58,** 58–59
Fool's gold. see Pyrite
Fossils 18, 24, **24,** 80, **80,** 86; see also Amber; Petrified wood
Fuji, Mount, Japan 21, **21**

## G

Gabbro 72–73, 74
Galápagos Islands, South Pacific Ocean 75, **75**
Galena 41, **42, 43,** 51, 52, **52**
Garnet 15, **62,** 101, 103
Gaspeite 55, **55**
Gemstones 61, **62–63,** 79, 81, 101
Geodes 36, **36,** 59, 61
Giant's Causeway, Northern Ireland 71, **71**
Global Positioning System (GPS) 10, 32, **33,** 68, 77, 103
Gneiss 68, **87,** 87–88
Gold 22, 37, 38, 40, 41, 43, 48, 51, 52, 101
Grand Canyon, Arizona, U.S.A. **80,** 81
Granite 72
  as building material 73, 94, 98, 99, 100, 103
  carvings 73, **73**
  close-up **74**
  crystals 70, 76
Graphite **35,** 37, 50, 74, 103
Gypsum **35, 45,** 56, 80, 82, 84, 86, 98, 103

## H

Halides 48, 58–59
Halite. see Salt
Health: and minerals 37, 101–102
Hematite 39, 40, **41,** 52, 53, **53,** 98, 99
Hornfels 88, **88**

## I

Ice 25, **25,** 34, 53
Igneous rocks 23, **24,** 26, 70, 72–76, 79

## J

Jade 60, **60**
Jet 61, **61**

## K

Kaolinite 40, **40**
Kenya **6,** 96, **97**
Kestrels 23, **23**
Kimberlite 73, 74, **74,** 75
Kyanite **35,** 41, 43

## L

Lapis lazuli 86, **86,** 99, 100
Lava, cooled: close-up **75**
Lava domes 21, **21**
Lava flows 20, 77, 79
Limestone 24, 82–84, **84,** 86, 88, 94, 98, 99, 100
Limonite 43, **43,** 99
Lithosphere 14, 17–19, 23, 27, 76

**M**
Mad Hatter (character) 102, **102**
Madagascar 32, **33**
Magma
　crystal growth 34
　explosions 20, 74
　ingredients 20, 70
　rock cycle **26,** 26–27
　temperatures 70
Magnetite 14, **14,** 43, 98
Malachite 39, 40, **41,** 54, 99
Marble 24, **24,** 88, **88,** 98, **99, 100**
Mars (planet) 53, **53,** 81, **81**
Mauna Kea (volcano), Hawaii, U.S.A. 21, **21**
Mercury (element) 25, **25,** 53, 102, **102**
Metals 12, 13, 39, 43, 48, 52
Metamorphic rocks 24, 26, 86–88
Meteorites 12, **14,** 72, **89,** 89–91, **90–91**
Mica 41, 42, 72, 81, 87, 88
Minerals
　characteristics 37–38
　chemical formulas 46–47, 48
　classification system 48
　cleavage 41–42, **42**
　color 38, 39
　fracture 42–43
　hardness 44, 45
　luster 40
　major groups 48, 50–51, 53–61
　oddities 25, **25**
　properties 38, 40–44
　specific gravity 43
　streak 40–41, **41**
　what they are 22
Mines and mining 23, 32, 52, **52**
Mohs, Friedrich 44, **44**
Mohs scale 44, 45
Molten rock **12,** 13, 17, 19, 20, **20**

**N**
Native elements 48–50
Nebulae 12, **12,** 89
Nonmetals 48, 50

**O**
Obsidian 25, **25,** 43, 75–76, **76**
Ol Doinyo Lengai (volcano), Tanzania 7, 10, **11**
Ol Pejeta Conservancy, Kenya 96, **97**
Olivine 15, **15, 72,** 73, 89
Oxides 48, 53–54

**P**
Paint: from rocks and minerals 53, 55, 86, 98–99; make your own 104–105, **104–105**
Pangaea (supercontinent) 18, **18**
Pegmatite 73
Peridot **62,** 89
Peridotite 16, 73–74, 75
Periodic table 46–47, **46–47**
Petrified wood 85, **85**
Phosphates 48, 57
Phosphorus 49, **49,** 50, 57
Pigments 53, 55, 102, 105
Planets 12–13, **13,** 15; see also Earth; Mars
Plate tectonics 18–19, 26–27, **27,** 68
Pumice 20, 74, 76, **76**
Puy de Dôme volcanoes, France 21, **21**
Pyramids: Egypt **94–95,** 100
Pyrite 35, **35,** 38, 40, 41, 43, **50–51,** 51
Pyromorphite 57, **57**

**Q**
Quartz
　crystals **40, 45,** 85, 86, 103
　geodes 36
　hardness test **44**
　properties 38, 40, 43, 44, 45, 60–61
　uses 98, 103
Quartzite 88

**R**
Rhyolite 76, 79
Ring of Fire 20, **20**

Rock paint 104–105, **104–105**
Rocks
　felsic vs. mafic 74, **74**
　igneous 23, 26, **26,** 70, 72–75, 79
　metamorphic 24, **24,** 26, **26,** 86–88
　oddities 25, **25**
　rock cycle **26,** 26
　sedimentary 24, **24,** 26, **26,** 78, **78,** 79–86
　from space 89, 90–91, **90–91**
　what they are 23
Rubies 38, 61, **63**
Rushmore, Mount, South Dakota, U.S.A. 73, **73**

**S**
Salt
　chemical formula 46, **46**
　crystals 22, **22,** 34, 42, 82
　formations 58, **58**
　rock salt 42, 82, 84
　table salt 46, **46,** 58, 82
Sandstone 80–81, 88, 104, **104**
　canyons **8–9, 80,** 81
　rock formations **2–3,** 78
Sapphires 38, **38,** 54, 62, **62,** 73
Schist 87–88
Sedimentary rocks 24, 26, **26, 78,** 79–84, 86
Seismic waves 17, **17**
Semimetals 48, 50
Serengeti National Park, Tanzania 68, **69**
Shale 80, 81, **81,** 87, 88
Shield volcanoes 21, **21,** 75
Silica 74, 75, 76, 80, 86
Silicates 15, 48, 59–60
Silicon: used in electronics 50, **50**
Silver 40, 51, 98, 101, 102
Slate 87, **87,** 98
Solar system 13, **13,** 89
Stalactites and stalagmites 83, **83**
The Starry Night (van Gogh) 86, **86**
Sugar 37, **37,** 64, **64,** 65
Sulfates 48, 56
Sulfides 48, 50–51, 53
Sulfur 50–51

**T**
Taj Mahal, Agra, India 100, **100**
Talc 44, **45,** 60
Tanzania 7, 10, **11,** 68, **69**
Tanzanite 63
Tectonic plates 19–20, 27, **27,** 68, 86, 87
Tinnunculite 23, **23**
Topaz **35,** 44, **45,** 60, **60,** 63
Tourmaline **63,** 73
Tufa towers 82, **82**
Tuff 79, 99, **99**
Turquoise **57,** 57

**U**
Ultraviolet light 59, **59**
Universe: big bang 12

**V**
Volcanic ash 77, **77**
Volcanic glass **25,** 75, 76, **76**
Volcano, make your own 28–29, **28–29**
Volcanoes
　eruptions 10, **11,** 20, 77, **77,** 79
　facts 20
　types of 21, **21**
　underwater 20, 75

**W**
Wavellite 57, **57**
Wegener, Alfred 18

**X**
Xenoliths 74, 75

**Y**
Yucatán Peninsula, Mexico: crater 91

**Z**
Zinc 37, 48, 101
Zircon **35,** 40

# CREDITS

ASP: Alamy Stock Photo; DT: Dreamstime; GI: Getty Images; IS: iStock; NGIC: National Geographic Image Collection; SCI: Science Source; SS: Shutterstock

Cover (gold), Eli Maier/SS; (stones), mariakraynova/SS; (green), Richard Leeney/Dorling Kindersley/GI; (various diamonds), Mishatc/DT; (purple), Greg C Grace/ASP; (red), Fuse/GI; (orange), The Natural History Museum/ASP; (arch), John A Davis/SS; (expert), Courtesy Dr. Sarah Stamps; (diamond group), oneo/SS; (fossil), Dinoton/SS; (geode), movit/SS; Spine (green), Richard Leeney/Dorling Kindersley/GI; Back cover, Vinicius Bacarin/SS; 1, Edwin Verin/SS; 2-3, francescoriccardoiacomino/SS; 4 (UP), MarcelClemens/SS; 4 (LE), In The Light Photography/SS; 4 (RT), YamabikaY/SS; 4 (sapphire), Pisut Phaetrangsee/SS; 4 (garnet), STUDIO492/SS; 4-5 (gems), J. Palys/SS; 5 (UP), Dinoton/SS; 5 (LE), Byelikova Oksana/SS; 5 (RT), Pius Lee/SS; 5 (LO), TinaImages/SS; 6 (UP), Dr. Sarah Stamps; 7 (UP), Dr. Sarah Stamps; 10 (UP), Dr. Sarah Stamps; 8-9, In The Light Photography/SS; 10 (LO), Bjoern Wylezich/SS; 11 (UP LE), Niels Busch/GI; 11 (UP RT), Bjoern Wylezich/SS; 11 (LO), Dr. Sarah Stamps; 12 (LE), Dimitri Goderdzishvili/SS; 12 (RT), Robert Crow/SS; 13 (UP), cigdem/SS; 13 (LO), Roman Samokhin/SS; 14 (UP), Ana Del Castillo/DT; 14 (LO), Pyty/SS; 15 (UP), crazydiva/IS; 15 (LO), Bonita R. Cheshier/SS; 16, Andrea Danti/SS; 17 (UP), Belish/SS; 17 (LO), Daniel Kreher/GI; 18 (UP), Designua/SS; 18 (LO), Designua/SS; 19 (UP), Daniel Prudek/SS; 19 (LO), Nido Huebl/SS; 20 (UP), T.Thinnapat/SS; 20 (LO), NG Maps; 21 (UP), Chris Bickford/NGIC; 21 (UP CTR), Videowokart/SS; 21 (LO CTR), Cormon Francis/hemis.fr/GI; 21 (LO), Marisa Estivill/SS; 22 (UP), Maria Sbytova/SS; 22 (LO), Jeff Holcombe/SS; 23 (UP LE), Narupon Nimpaiboon/SS; 23 (UP RT), Tom Mortimer; 24 (UP), Wildnerdpix/SS; 24 (CTR), MarcelClemens/SS; 24 (LO), Walter Bilotta/SS; 24 (LO CTR), vvoe/SS; 24 (LO LE), ntv/SS; 25 (UP LE), MarcelClemens/SS; 25 (UP RT), GaryTalton/IS; 25 (LO RT), Madlen/SS; 26 (UP RT), Tyler Boyes/SS; 26 (CTR), bogdan ionescu/SS; 26 (LO LE), milart/SS; 26 (LO RT), elenaburn/SS; 27 (UP), Poelzer Wolfgang/ASP; 27 (LO), Designua/SS; 28 (UP), Vitalii Gaidukov/SS; 28 (LO), JGI/Jamie Grill/GI; 29, (tray), little birdie/SS; (baking soda), Gts/SS; (bowl), nito/SS; (brushes), Africa Studio/SS; (clay), xpixel/SS; (dye), Elizabeth A.Cummings/SS; (foil), ronstik/SS; (funnel), wk1003mike/SS; (jar), Sergieiev/SS; (soap), stuar/SS; (animals), Marek Szumlas/SS; (vinegar), Pat_Hastings/SS; 30-31, YamabikaY/SS; 32 (UP), Dr. Sarah Stamps; 32 (LO), Bjoern Wylezich/SS; 33 (UP LE), Dr. Sarah Stamps; 33 (UP RT), Bjoern Wylezich/SS; 33 (LO), Dr. Sarah Stamps; 34, Breck P. Kent/SS; 35 (UP LE), Anneka/SS; 35 (UP RT), Albert Russ/SS; 35 (CTR LE), Coldmoon Photoproject/SS; 35 (CTR), carlosdelacalle/SS; 35 (LO LE), Cagla Acikgoz/SS; 35 (LO RT), Breck P. Kent/SS; 36 (UP), Paul Dymond/GI; 36 (LO), Patricia Chumillas/SS; 37, Gayvoronskaya_Yana/SS; 38 (LO LE), gorosan/SS; 38 (LO RT), Epitavi/SS; 39 (UP), Joanne Dunbar/SS; 39 (LO LE), Stefan Dinse/DT; 39 (LO RT), Carlosphotos/DT; 40 (CTR), Robert D Pinna/SS; 40 (LO), Aleksandr Pobedimskiy/SS; 41 (LO), Tyler Boyes/SS; 41 (UP), Joel Arem/GI; 42 (UP), Jiri Vaclavek/SS; 42 (CTR), Linnas/SS; 42 (LO), Christopher PB/SS; 43 (UP), Eduardo Estellez/SS; 43 (LO), Albert Russ/SS; 44 (LE), bilwissedition Ltd. & Co. KG/ASP; 44 (LO RT), Joel Arem/GI; 45, (calcite), Roy Palmer/SS; (diamond), LifetimeStock/SS; (gypsum, fluorite, apatite, feldspar, corundum), Aleksandr Pobedimskiy/SS; (penny), rsooll/SS; (quartz), Ekaterina Fribus/DT; (talc), Manamana/SS; (topaz), Albert Russ/SS; 46, KITTI_PHIT/SS; 46-47 (LO), julie deshaies/SS; 47 (UP), robert_s/SS; 48, NLM/Science Source; 49 (UP), VCG/VCG/GI; 49 (CTR), Konstantin Yolshin/SS; 49 (LO), maximimages.com/ASP; 50 (CTR), MS Mikel/SS; 50 (LO), Highwaystarz-Photography/IS; 50-51 (LO), NataliyaF/SS; 51 (CTR), Recep-Bg/GI; 51 (LO RT), SunnyChinchilla/SS; 52 (LO), Vitaly Raduntsev/SS; 52 (UP), Lee Prince/SS; 53 (LO), Jeremy Red/SS; 53 (UP), NASA/JPL-Caltech/Cornell/USGS; 54 (UP), Albert Russ/SS; 54 (CTR), Gunnerchu/SS; 54-55 (UP), Potapov Alexander/SS; 55 (UP), Igor Tichonow/SS; 55 (CTR), elroyspelbos/SS; 56 (UP), Albert Russ/SS; 56 (LO), Claudio Briones/SS; 56-57 (LO), Wisconsinart/DT; 57 (UP), Roy Palmer/SS; 57 (LO), Albert Russ/SS; 58 (UP), Vadim Petrakov/SS; 58 (LO), Cagla Acikgoz/SS; 59 (CTR), Gabbro/ASP; 59 (LO), Breck P. Kent/SS; 60 (LE), Fred S. Pinheiro/SS; 60 (RT), ChameleonsEye/SS; 61 (UP), J. Palys/SS; 61 (LO LE), Yuriy Buyvol/SS; 61 (LO RT), vvoe/SS; 62 (diamond), everything possible/SS; (emerald), boykung/SS; (garnet), STUDIO492/SS; (peridot), Epitavi/SS; (sapphire), Pisut Phaetrangsee/SS; (alexandrite), boykung/SS; (amethyst), Boris Sosnovyy/SS; (aquamarine), TinaImages/SS; (citrine), Nastya22/SS; (ruby), Potapov Alexander/SS; (tanzanite), PNSJ88/SS; (tourmaline), J. Palys/SS; 64 (UP), JeniFoto/SS; 64 (CTR), Simon Watson/GI; 64 (LE), Christophe Testi/DT; 64 (LO), Dynamicfoto/SS; 65 (UP LE), Scott Bolster/SS; 65 (UP RT), Madlen/SS; 65 (RT), Naruedom Yaempongsa/SS; 65 (LO LE), Sergieiev/SS; 66-67, Byelikova Oksana/SS; 68 (UP), Dr. Sarah Stamps; 69 (LO), Victor Lapaev/SS; 69 (UP LE), Georgia Evans/SS; 69 (UP RT), Bjoern Wylezich/SS; 70, Gianni Dagli Orti/SS; 71 (UP), S-F/SS; 71 (LO), Historica Graphica Collection/Heritage Images/GI; 72 (UP), Matteo Chinellato-ChinellatoPhoto/SS; 72 (CTR), Dennis Hardley/ASP; 72 (LO), Moha El-Jaw/SS; 73, Greg and Jan Ritchie/SS; 74 (UP), Bryan Chute/DT; 74 (UP CTR), Valery Kraynov/SS; 74 (LO), Bjoern Wylezich/SS; 75 (UP), Andrew Plumptre/GI; 75 (LO), Kletr/SS; 76 (UP), Rob Kemp/SS; 76 (LO), Vitaliy Balenko/SS; 77 (UP LE), andersen_oystein/IS; 77 (UP RT), Bychkov Kirill/SS; 78 (UP), NPS/Neal Herbert; 78 (LO), PrapatsThai/SS; 79, Cegli/SS; 80 (UP), sumikophoto/SS; 80 (LO), BGSmith/SS; 81 (UP LE), Ievgen Kryshen/SS; 81 (UP RT), NASA/JPL-Caltech/MSSS; 81 (LO), VvoeVale/IS; 82 (CTR), Marius Sipa/DT; 82 (LO), Oliclimb/DT; 83, Vinicius Bacarin/SS; 84 (UP), Fokinol/DT; 84 (LO), Shtraus Dmytro/SS; 85, Felix Lipov/SS; 86 (UP), George W. Bailey/SS; 86 (LO LE), J. Palys/SS; 86 (LO RT), Niday Picture Library/ASP; 87 (LO LE), Jean Williamson/ASP; 87 (LO RT), northlightimages/IS; 88 (LO LE), lazyllama/SS; 88 (LO RT), De Agostini Picture Library/GI; 89, De Agostini Picture Library/GI; 90 (UP), Dennis K. Johnson/GI; 90 (CTR), Migel/SS; 90 (LO), Herval Freire; 91 (UP), Mark Garlick/Science Source; 91 (LO), Action Sports Photography/SS; 92 (chert), Tyler Boyes/SS; (conglomerate), Fokinol/DT; (cups), Yuliyan Velchev/SS; (glue), Mega Pixel/SS; (pen), Sergej Razvodovskij/SS; (shells), Whiteaster/SS; (soil), rodimov/SS; 93, Yuliyan Velchev/SS; 94-95 (RT), Pius Lee/SS; 96 (UP), Dr. Sarah Stamps; 96 (LO), Bjoern Wylezich/SS; 97 (UP LE), Dr. Sarah Stamps; 97 (UP RT), Bjoern Wylezich/SS; 97 (LO), Jiri Balek/SS; 98 (LO LE), KPixMining/SS; 98-99, Songquan Deng/SS; 99 (UP), Ruslan Gilmanshin/DT; 99 (LO RT), Viktor Gmyria/DT; 100, Byelikova Oksana/SS; 101 (UP), JGI/Jamie Grill/GI; 101 (LO LE), Fotokon/DT; 101 (LO RT), K.Decha/SS; 102 (UP), Morphart Creation/SS; 102 (CTR), Marcel Clemens/DT; 103 (UP), Vadim Ratnikov/SS; 103 (LO), awayge/IS; 104 (UP), STILLFX/SS; 104 (CTR), Westend61/GI; 104 (LO LE), Aleksandr Pobedimskiy/SS; 104 (LO RT), Fokinol/DT; 105 (goggles), Shakeyimages/DT; (hammer), Volkop/DT; (towel), Yuthana Choradet Ness/SS; (pitcher), Runrun2/SS; (morter), NGS; (painting), monkeybusinessimages/IS; 107, Kagai19927/SS

For young rock hounds everywhere. —RS

Since 1888, the National Geographic Society has funded more than 12,000 research, exploration, and preservation projects around the world. The Society receives funds from National Geographic Partners, LLC, funded in part by your purchase. A portion of the proceeds from this book supports this vital work. To learn more, visit natgeo.com/info.

For more information, visit nationalgeographic.com, call 1-800-647-5463, or write to the following address:

National Geographic Partners
1145 17th Street N.W.
Washington, D.C. 20036-4688 U.S.A.

Visit us online at nationalgeographic.com/books

For librarians and teachers: ngchildrensbooks.org

More for kids from National Geographic: natgeokids.com

*National Geographic Kids* magazine inspires children to explore their world with fun yet educational articles on animals, science, nature, and more. Using fresh storytelling and amazing photography, *Nat Geo Kids* shows kids ages 6 to 14 the fascinating truth about the world—and why they should care. **kids.nationalgeographic.com/subscribe**

For information about special discounts for bulk purchases, please contact National Geographic Books Special Sales: specialsales@natgeo.com

For rights or permissions inquiries, please contact National Geographic Books Subsidiary Rights: bookrights@natgeo.com

Designed by Girl Friday Productions

All information provided by Dr. Stamps are of her opinion and do not reflect the opinion of Virginia Tech.

The authors and publisher also wish to thank the book team: Priyanka Lamichhane, project editor; Amanda Larsen, art director; Sarah J. Mock, photo editor; Molly Reid, production editor.

**Library of Congress Cataloging-in-Publication Data**

Names: Strother, Ruth, author. | National Geographic Society (U.S.)
Title: Rocks and minerals / by Ruth Strother.
Other titles: Absolute expert.
Description: Washington, DC : National Geographic Kids, [2019] | Series: Absolute expert | Audience: Ages 8-12. | Audience: Grades 4 to 6.
Identifiers: LCCN 2018031445| ISBN 9781426332791 (hardcover : alk. paper) | ISBN 9781426332807 (hardcover : alk. paper)
Subjects: LCSH: Rocks--Juvenile literature. | Minerals--Juvenile literature. | Earth (Planet)--Origin--Juvenile literature.
Classification: LCC QE432.2 .S78 2019 | DDC 552--dc23
LC record available at https://lccn.loc.gov/2018031445

Printed in China
19/RRDS/1

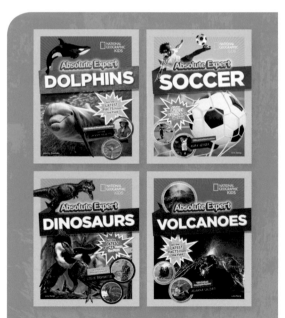